THE BEDFORD SERIES IN HISTORY AND CULTURE

Slavery, Freedom, and the Law in the Atlantic World

A Brief History with Documents

Related Titles in
THE BEDFORD SERIES IN HISTORY AND CULTURE
Advisory Editors: Lynn Hunt, *University of California, Los Angeles*
David W. Blight, *Yale University*
Bonnie G. Smith, *Rutgers University*
Natalie Zemon Davis, *Princeton University*
Ernest R. May, *Harvard University*

THE BEDFORD SERIES IN HISTORY AND CULTURE

Slavery, Freedom, and the Law in the Atlantic World

A Brief History with Documents

Sue Peabody

Washington State University Vancouver

Keila Grinberg

Universidade Federal do Estado do Rio de Janeiro

BEDFORD/ST. MARTIN'S   Boston ♦ New York

For Bedford/St. Martin's

Publisher for History: Mary V. Dougherty
Executive Editor for History: Katherine Meisenheimer
Director of Development for History: Jane Knetzger
Developmental Editor: Katie Janssen
Editorial Assistant: Laurel Damashek
Production Supervisor: Jennifer Peterson
Production Associate: Maureen O'Neill
Executive Marketing Manager: Jenna Bookin Barry
Project Management: Books By Design, Inc.
Text Design: Claire Seng-Niemoeller
Indexing: Books By Design, Inc.
Cover Design: Liz Tardiff
Cover Art: Agostino Brunias, "Pacification with the Maroon Negroes," in Bryan
    Edwards, *History Civil and Commercial of the British West Indies*, third edition
    (London: John Stockdale, 1801). Courtesy of Special Collections, University of
    Colorado at Boulder Libraries.
Composition: Stratford Publishing Services, Inc.
Printing and Binding: RR Donnelley & Sons Company

President: Joan E. Feinberg
Editorial Director: Denise B. Wydra
Director of Marketing: Karen Melton Soeltz
Director of Editing, Design, and Production: Marcia Cohen
Manager, Publishing Services: Emily Berleth

Library of Congress Control Number: 2006934044

Manufactured in the United States of America.

2   1   0   9   8
f   e   d   c   b

For information, write: Bedford/St. Martin's, 75 Arlington Street, Boston, MA 02116
(617-399-4000)

ISBN-10: 0-312-41176-6 (paperback)
ISBN-10: 0-4039-7151-X (hardcover)
ISBN-13: 978-0-312-41176-3

Distributed outside the United States by Palgrave Macmillan.

Acknowledgments

Map of the Atlantic World (pp. xx–xxi): Courtesy of University of Colorado at Boulder
    Libraries, Boulder, Colo.
Document 11: Reprinted by permission of Higginson Book Company.
Document 15, Document 17: Reprinted with the permission of LexisNexis.
Document 28: Reprinted by permission of Carlos Aguirre.
Document 44: Reprinted by permission of Robert Conrad.

Foreword

The Bedford Series in History and Culture is designed so that readers can study the past as historians do.

The historian's first task is finding the evidence. Documents, letters, memoirs, interviews, pictures, movies, novels, or poems can provide facts and clues. Then the historian questions and compares the sources. There is more to do than in a courtroom, for hearsay evidence is welcome, and the historian is usually looking for answers beyond act and motive. Different views of an event may be as important as a single verdict. How a story is told may yield as much information as what it says.

Along the way the historian seeks help from other historians and perhaps from specialists in other disciplines. Finally, it is time to write, to decide on an interpretation and how to arrange the evidence for readers.

Each book in this series contains an important historical document or group of documents, each document a witness from the past and open to interpretation in different ways. The documents are combined with some element of historical narrative—an introduction or a biographical essay, for example—that provides students with an analysis of the primary source material and important background information about the world in which it was produced.

Each book in the series focuses on a specific topic within a specific historical period. Each provides a basis for lively thought and discussion about several aspects of the topic and the historian's role. Each is short enough (and inexpensive enough) to be a reasonable one-week assignment in a college course. Whether as classroom or personal reading, each book in the series provides firsthand experience of the challenge—and fun—of discovering, recreating, and interpreting the past.

Lynn Hunt
David W. Blight
Bonnie G. Smith
Natalie Zemon Davis
Ernest R. May

Preface

Designed for use in college courses, this book gives readers firsthand accounts of slaves' lawsuits for freedom during the rapidly changing periods of plantation slavery, national independence, and abolition. While some of the earliest texts we include provide a legal background for sixteenth- to early eighteenth-century slavery, most documents concentrate on the late eighteenth and nineteenth centuries, when the new United States, Haiti, and Latin American nations struggled for independence and attempted to define the emerging categories of citizenship, often linked to race. In these emergent nations, the history of dependence on slave labor, coupled with new rhetorics and ideologies based on the volatile and contested notion of freedom, yielded profound and sometimes violent contradictions that are reflected in court records.

The laws, petitions, judicial decisions, and other legal documents in this book—most translated into accessible English for the first time—are organized within French, English, Spanish, and Portuguese imperial chapters. Because this book traces the history of legally sanctioned freedom, we begin with the French Empire, where the very name of France meant "freedom" and the slaves of Saint-Domingue forced general emancipation during the Haitian Revolution. The chapter on England, the British West Indies, and the United States follows, with documents from the famous *Somerset* case, the abolition of the slave trade, and the abolition of slavery in the British Empire and the United States. Although the Portuguese and Spanish societies' involvement with slavery dates from the Roman and Islamic periods, Cuba and Brazil were the last to abolish chattel slavery in the nineteenth century, and so we conclude here. The Spanish chapter moves from the medieval Spanish legal code, *Las Siete Partidas*, to the rapid intensification of plantation slavery in colonial Cuba, independent Ecuador, and Peru, as well as the tradition of *coartación* (self-purchase) and the establishment of free soil in Spain. The chapter on Portugal and Brazil traces the laws regulating slavery and freedom as well as numerous cases in Brazil wherein slaves negotiated the terms of their freedom. The epilogue, written by Rebecca Scott of the University of Michigan and Daniel Nemser of the University of California, Berkeley, with the assistance of Orlando García Martínez of the Archivo Histórico Provincial de Cienfuegos, Cuba, shows how former slaves used judicial courts to demand reparations for slavery in early twentieth-century Cuba.

The introductory essay sets these documents in the larger unfolding history of slavery and emancipation in the Atlantic World. We emphasize the range of experiences for slaves and free people, based upon local context, economic pressures, and political traditions. Separate sections treat the practice of slavery and traditions of freedom in the French, English, Spanish, and Portuguese empires, including national independence for Haiti, the United States, Peru, Cuba, and Brazil.

In addition to these documents, *Slavery, Freedom, and the Law* includes original illustrations that evoke the lived experience of slaves as well as their representation in historical media, such as travelogues, newspapers, and abolitionist tracts. A brief headnote contextualizes each visual and written document. In addition, we have included a chronology of important dates in the history of slavery and abolition, discussion questions, a bibliography for further reading, a map of the Atlantic World with African, European, and American cities and locales referenced in the text, and an index.

ACKNOWLEDGMENTS

A work of such broad range and diverse parts is the product of many hands. First, we would like to thank Rebecca Scott, who generously suggested the project, seeded it with the wonderful document that constitutes our epilogue, and, not least of all, introduced us to one another. Keila and Sue collaborated on this project for more than a year via the miracle of the Internet before meeting face to face; Rebecca's good instincts have yielded not only a fruitful academic partnership but also a wonderful friendship.

Yale University's Gilder Lehrman Center for the Study of Slavery and Abolition supported some of Sue Peabody's research for this project. Washington State University Vancouver supported the translation and research fees with an Internal Research Mini-Grant. The Brazilian National Council for Scientific and Technological Development (CNPq) and CAPES/Ministry of Education in Brazil supported some of Keila Grinberg's research.

Readers' and reviewers' expertise and generous suggestions improved this book tremendously. We especially wish to thank six reviewers of the original manuscript—Carlos Aguirre, University of Oregon; Laurent Dubois, Michigan State University; Paul Finkelman, Albany Law School; Steven Mintz, University of Houston; Pamela Scully, Emory University; and Steve Whitman, Mount St. Mary's University—whose thoughtful, encouraging, and close reading of earlier drafts helped us not only to correct our errors but also to see broader connections, making this a much better book than we could have produced on our own. In addition, we would like to thank others who have encouraged us, pointing to documents, images, and histories that have enriched this work, especially Carlo A. Célius, Université Laval; David Brion Davis, Yale University; Alejandro de la Fuente, University of Pittsburgh; Seymour Drescher, University of Pittsburgh; David Eltis, Queens University; John Garrigus, University of Texas at Arlington; Daniel Hulsebosch, New York University; Silvia Hunold Lara, Universidade Estadual de Campinas; Melanie Newton, University of Toronto; Diana Paton, University of Newcastle; Richard Price, College of William and Mary; Leslie Rowland, University of Maryland; and Mimi Sheller, Lancaster University.

Working with rare documents requires additional help from the good librarians at many institutions, including Tami Gierloff, Associate Director, Boley Law Library, Lewis and Clark University; Kris McCusker of Special Collections Department, University of Colorado at Boulder libraries; Diane Windham Shaw of Special Collections, Skillman Library, Lafayette College; and Lynda Corey Claassen, Director of the Mandeville Special Collections Library, University of California San Diego. Rebecca Scott would like to convey special thanks to Orlando García Martínez, former director of the Archivo Histórico Provincial de Cienfuegos, who located the transcript of the lawsuit by Andrea Quesada.

Colleagues, staff, and students at our respective institutions have contributed to this book in important ways. At Washington State University, Nicole Campbell, Reference Librarian and Electronic Resources Coordinator, worked with Sue Peabody and her students as they identified, located, and "test ran" the documents. Marie Kojis Pham and Mary Stuart, students extraordinaires, worked as research assistants on this project. Leslie Wykoff, Karen Diller, and Kerry Hodges supported this research with unusual dedication to acquisitions and cheerful support. We relied heavily on Linda Frederiksen's intrepid interlibrary loan expertise. Shari Clevenger and Jeannette Altman brought their sharp eyes and good humor to the scanning of images.

Sue's students in the History and Honors Seminars on Slavery, Freedom, and the Law helped us decide what worked and what didn't and ultimately suggested several documents that found their way into this book.

Bedford/St. Martin's has been a terrific press to work with from the beginning. Natalie Zemon Davis and Lynn Hunt, two French historians who inspired us to work with legal records at the outset of our careers, encouraged our pursuit of this project. A succession of fine editors smoothly brought the book to fruition, including Patricia Rossi, Katherine Meisenheimer, Mary Dougherty, and ultimately Jane Knetzger, who deserves the credit for midwifery at the end. We especially want to thank Katie Janssen, who brought luster, precision, and style to our prose and was fun and funny as well. We are grateful to Carina Schoenberger and Shannon Hunt, who assisted at the beginning, and to Laurel Damashek, Emily Berleth, and Nancy Benjamin for their help with the final production.

Our translators deserve special thanks. John Michael Corley brought years of experience and wisdom to his translations of the Spanish documents; thanks to Sherie for loaning him to us. Mark William Lutes, a Brazilian soul born by mistake in Canada, devoted hours of his precious time to translating the Portuguese documents. Special thanks to Daniel Nemser of the University of California at Berkeley, who worked with Rebecca Scott to produce a precise translation of excerpts from the court record.

Sue thanks Keila for five years of enjoyable work and friendship, including laughter, inspiration, collegiality, dreams, and visits. You bring out the best in me.

Keila also thanks Sue for the wonderful and rare combination of friendship, work, and academic collaboration. Thanks for showing up on my computer five years ago.

Finally, we want to thank our respective families, without whom life would be unimaginable and who sacrifice a great deal to see us work so much. Sue thanks Scott Hewitt, for patience, generosity, humor, and a razzy hat; Miles Hewitt, a star in class and on the court; Louise Hewitt, tender, generous, and creative. Keila thanks Flavio Limoncic every day for being so patient and good-humored. Tatiana and Carolina were both born in the making of this book—Keila thanks them for the joy in their eyes and for never letting her work on weekends.

Sue Peabody
Keila Grinberg

A Note about Editing, Translation, and Racial Terminology

The goal of editing and translating the documents in this book has been to make their contents understandable and interesting to undergraduate students today while remaining as faithful as possible to the alien world of the past. To this end, we favored a looser, more colloquial style whenever it did not do violence to the differences of the historical context. Punctuation and capitalization were modernized; lengthy documents were edited down for brevity and clarity. At the same time, certain unfamiliar terms (for example, monetary units, social categories) were retained when we felt that the unfamiliar terms best convey the reality or the mind-set of the historical people who created these documents.

Racial terminology is an especially sensitive area for the historian and student alike. In general, we used the terms *black* and *African American* more or less interchangeably in our own prose, with *American* understood to apply to inhabitants of the entire South and North American continents, as well as the islands of the Caribbean. When quoting English-language historical documents, we used the original terminology of those documents, such as *Negro* and *colored*. It is important to understand that for many people today these terms carry with them connotations of disrespect and ought not to be used—except to quote others—in discussions, papers, or even private conversations. The more respectful terms, growing out of the U.S. civil rights movement, are *black* and *African American*.

Translating racial terminology from French, Spanish, and Portuguese documents posed more of a challenge. The migration of thousands of Africans and Europeans to the Americas—especially as men outnumbered women in many of these colonial settlements—led inevitably to children with mixed Native American, European, and African lineage. The terms used to mark people of mixed lineage varied quite a bit between language groups and even within them. In the

United States, especially in places where British colonists dominated, racial categories were often applied with stark contrast: A person was "black" or "white" or occasionally "mulatto." But in many Atlantic societies, a more finely calibrated vocabulary of distinction emerged. For example, one French writer claimed that eleven different words (*blanc, sang-mêlé, quarteronné, mamelouc, métis, quarteron, mulâtre, marabou, griffe, sacatra, noir*) were necessary to represent the relative proportion of black and white ancestry of colonial subjects in the French colony of Saint-Domingue (today, Haiti), going back seven generations. Collectively, people of African ancestry, especially those who also had European ancestry, were known as *gens de couleur* ("people of color"). All of these terms, with the exception of *noir*, are considered impolite in France today. In Spanish America, where indigenous Americans made up a much greater proportion of most colonial populations, racial terminology focused on miscegenation (racial mixing) between whites and Native Americans (for example, *mestizo*) and was often influenced by conformity to cultural and social norms, such as dress and language.

Generally, we tried to use English terms that are roughly equivalent to those of the original language. For example, we substituted the English word *Negro* for the French *nègre*. This, however, is not quite an accurate translation, since the term *nègre* also connoted slave status in the eighteenth century, not just color. Sometimes we elected to retain certain antiquated terms—for example, *Negress*, as opposed to the more contemporary *black woman*—because it gives something more of the flavor of the original text.

Contents

Illustrations

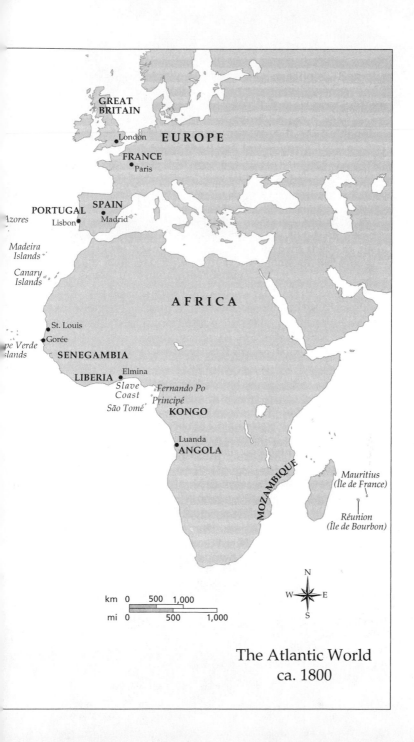

The Atlantic World
ca. 1800

PART ONE

Introduction: Slavery, Freedom, and the Law

What is the difference between slavery and freedom? In twenty-first-century culture, these concepts are so ingrained in our thinking—the first imagined as an absolute evil and the other as a self-evident good—that we view this question as only an abstract philosophical dilemma. We rarely stop to wonder what *slavery* and *freedom* mean in concrete terms.

For the people who lived in the Atlantic World between 1700 and 1900—the millions of individuals whose lives were shaped by the crisscrossing social, economic, political, and cultural relationships between Africans, Europeans, and indigenous Americans—differentiating between slavery and freedom was central to their lived experience. The Atlantic World was both hierarchical and highly mobile. People from Africa, Europe, and the Americas were connected with one another through military, political, social, sexual, commercial, and other kinds of transactions. Merchants, sailors, artisans, and officials, as well as manual laborers, prostitutes, laundresses, and apprentices, lived in port cities, the hubs of many Atlantic World exchanges. Rural workers on four Atlantic continents transformed the raw materials of agriculture and mining—corn and wheat, tobacco, sugarcane, cotton, indigo, furs, fish, gold, iron, silver—and even human beings into commodities whose value increased the farther they traveled from their points of origin.

The social and legal ties that bound workers to their labor and to their masters varied over time and place. (Note that the term *master* applied to both the supervisor of contract laborers—people like apprentices and indentured servants—and the owner of slaves.) Some bonded laborers worked with considerable autonomy, especially those panning for gold or hired out as day laborers because of their special skills. Others suffered under the constant supervision or violent force of the master or an overseer. Freedom and slavery, therefore, were not mirror opposites, but contained many gradations and social implications.

One of the most important sites where people thrashed out the meanings of slavery and freedom was in the judicial courts. Court cases created a rhetoric to describe slavery and freedom and had specific, physical consequences. Kings and politicians might pronounce laws, but when disputes arose, it was the judges and juries who ruled on them, creating immediate, tangible results in people's lives. Slaves and free people of color could in certain circumstances claim rights in court, framing their interests in a new, emerging language of citizenship, natural law, and humanity.

Legal documents offer a unique perspective into the motives, actions, and ideas of men and women on both sides of the shifting line between slavery and freedom. The documents in this book include lawyers' arguments, judges' decisions, notary acts, statutes, and even a treaty; they all shed light on how slaves and free people perceived the rights and privileges of freedom. They also reveal how courts and other institutions reinforced inequalities, sharpening hierarchies for slaves and free people alike.

The documents included here are presented chronologically within four groups, one for each of the most important European imperial powers that colonized the Americas from the fifteenth through the nineteenth centuries.[1] One might expect to find the Spanish and Portuguese empires covered first, since they were the first to establish

---

[1]Due to space constraints, Dutch involvement in Atlantic slavery has been omitted from this book. The Dutch played a key transitional role between the southern European powers of Spain and Portugal and the northern European powers of England and France. They invested and participated heavily in the slave trade (especially in the seventeenth century) and established several colonies in the Americas (New Amsterdam, Suriname) where slave labor was a significant presence. But by the late eighteenth and nineteenth centuries (the period on which this volume concentrates), the Dutch presence in the Atlantic World was considerably reduced.

colonies in the Americas in the fifteenth and sixteenth centuries and the first to transport slaves from Africa to the New World. Intensive English, French, and Dutch colonization and involvement in slavery came about later, in the early seventeenth century.

However, we decided to begin with the French chapter, followed by the English, Spanish, and Portuguese chapters. This is because our central theme is how legal institutions of the state manufactured and mediated the category of freedom in the dynamic period of Atlantic revolution, independence, and emancipation. Since freedom, rather than slavery, is the central theme of this collection, the French and English documents take precedence because the northern Atlantic is where new, dynamic concepts of freedom and the state were first forged. French judicial courts were the first to uphold and promote the Freedom Principle, the notion that simply setting foot on a particular territory was enough to confer freedom upon a slave. The slaves who rose in revolt in the French colony of Saint-Domingue during the 1790s forced the first general emancipation of a slave state (1793–1794) and the establishment of the first black republic in the world (Haiti, 1804). Abolitionism, the grassroots political movement to abolish slavery everywhere, arose first within the English empire. The radical egalitarianism of some Quakers and other humanitarians brought people of conscience to organize antislavery societies in England and the American colonies.

The Spanish and Portuguese Atlantic empires also innovated and mediated the meanings of freedom. Portugal embraced the notion of the Freedom Principle as it applied to the metropole (imperial center) in 1761, more than a decade before English abolitionists made it the cornerstone of their strategy. Even more importantly, both the Spanish and Portuguese empires upheld the uncodified practice of *coartación*, whereby a slave could purchase freedom over a period of time by paying installments on an agreed-upon price. In Spanish America, local governments upheld the slave's right to purchase his or her own freedom even over the master's objections, bringing freedom within the reach of a substantial minority of mostly urban Latin American slaves. *Coartación* reinforced the values of urban, merchant culture (hard work, thrift, delayed gratification) over the paternalistic, authoritarian regimes of the rural plantocracy.

European imperial powers did not have a monopoly on defining freedom. When the humiliation and violence of slavery became intolerable, some slaves seized their own freedom and escaped. In many colonial societies, slaves escaped individually or in small groups into swamps, canyons, or mountainous areas beyond European control and established independent communities. European colonists called these people "maroons" (from the Spanish word *cimarrón*, meaning domesticated cattle that had gone wild).

Maroon communities formed throughout North and South America and the Caribbean. They could be very small, made up of fewer than a dozen individuals, or much larger, including up to several thousand escaped slaves and their descendants. They posed a constant threat to the slaveholding regimes because they drew slaves away from the plantations and engaged in direct warfare against the planters. They flourished in the seventeenth and eighteenth centuries, when the Atlantic slave trade was at its most active. Most maroons were born in Africa and remembered their lives prior to enslavement; many fled shortly after they reached the New World. Others were creoles, born to enslaved parents in the Americas. Due to the sex imbalance of the Atlantic slave trade and the difficulties of living independently, maroons were predominantly young to middle-aged men, speaking African languages, practicing African religions and lifeways. Yet conditions in the Americas forced new practices too; the alien environments with unfamiliar plants and animals, the defensive military position vis-à-vis European-controlled settlements, the underrepresentation of women and children, and interactions with indigenous people all contributed to the development of a unique maroon identity.

Some maroon communities were so successful in establishing their independence and fighting off European colonists that the Europeans found it prudent to formally negotiate with them. Colonists established treaties with maroon leaders in Brazil, Colombia, Cuba, Ecuador, Hispaniola, Jamaica, Mexico, and Surinam, especially during the seventeenth and eighteenth centuries.

Before we explore the larger, transnational themes that emerge from studying these historical contexts side by side, it is worthwhile to pause and examine the historical trajectories of slavery and emancipation within each imperial context. For, while great variation emerged in the different European empires (ideas and practices regarding slavery and freedom in Massachusetts were very different from those in Georgia, to take one dramatic example), each national tradition (French, English, Spanish, and Portuguese) presents some cultural unity, particularly with regard to legal practices and precedents.

SLAVERY AND FREEDOM IN THE FRENCH ATLANTIC AND THE HAITIAN REVOLUTION

France was the last European power to enter the Atlantic game of conquest and colonization. In the first half of the seventeenth century, the French began a deliberate, sustained policy of exploration and colonization in American lands, resulting in the establishment of permanent settlements in what is now Canada, French Guiana (in South America), and the Caribbean islands of Martinique, Guadeloupe, and Saint-Domingue (Haiti). French settlements in Alabama and Louisiana came in the early eighteenth century.

The French initially invested in tobacco, following the English model, and employed French indentured servants to clear and work small plots of land. In the 1630s and 1640s, landholders increasingly turned to sugar cultivation, which required much larger plantations and a greater supply of labor to be profitable. French traders soon began to purchase slaves directly from West African suppliers. By the late seventeenth century, some 24,000 slaves outnumbered the 16,500 free people in the French colonies of the Caribbean. The size of the slave population prompted the king to issue a comprehensive slave law, the *Code Noir*, in 1685. (See Document 1.) The sovereign councils of Martinique, Guadeloupe, Saint-Christophe, and Saint-Domingue were responsible for publicizing and enforcing the law.

As its empire grew, the French government standardized the political bureaucracy of its overseas colonies. At the top was the king, and immediately beneath him was a secretary of state for the marine, both residing primarily in Versailles. The king appointed two royal officials to work directly in each colony: the governor, who was invariably a military officer from an old aristocratic family, and the intendant, who had financial and administrative oversight. The king's administrative structure deliberately pitted the two officers against one another, each watching his counterpart for corruption and misdeeds. Within the colonies, Superior Councils, consisting of six of the most prominent male colonists, were the highest judicial courts of appeal and generally represented the wealthiest slaveholders' interests. French colonial law emanated from the king's edicts and also from the colonial councils.

By the middle of the eighteenth century, France's empire extended virtually around the world. French settlers had established viable colonies from the northern reaches of Canada (Montreal, Quebec, Acadia) through the Mississippi basin of North America (Louisiana,

Saint Louis, Mobile) to the tropical Caribbean colonies (Martinique, Guadeloupe, Saint-Domingue, and French Guiana). In Africa, the French maintained a permanent presence in Senegal and traded for slaves in Guinea and Angola. France's connections to Asia were less robust, but two Indian Ocean island colonies, Île de France (Mauritius) and Île de Bourbon (Réunion), served merchants traveling to the French trading entrepôt in Pondichéry, along the southeastern coast of India, and eventually became plantation colonies similar to those in the Caribbean.

French colonists and merchants held slaves in all of these colonies, but the most important slave colonies were in and around the Caribbean. By 1750, slaves in Saint-Domingue (148,000), Martinique (66,000), Guadeloupe (43,000), and Louisiana (46,000) outnumbered the free population, in some cases by as much as ten to one. In Canada, Africa, and French India, by contrast, French merchants and residents might own several slaves as domestic servants, but they typically did not import large numbers of Africans to work plantations; slaves in these areas served more as status symbols than as productive laborers.

As the French empire became increasingly entangled with slavery, a legal problem emerged. France itself had no practical or legal tradition of slavery. In fact, several French cities, including Toulouse and Bordeaux, had ruled that slaves who entered their jurisdiction should be freed. By the eighteenth century, this Freedom Principle had been formalized and extended to the entire kingdom as the maxim "All persons are free in this kingdom, and as soon as a slave has arrived at the borders of this place, [the slave] is free."

But prosperous French colonists lobbied the government to allow them to bring their slaves across the Atlantic as servants. In 1716 and 1738, the king issued laws permitting slaveholders to bring their slaves to France for two purposes: religious instruction and training in a useful trade. The sum effect of these laws after 1738 was that slaveholders were required to obtain permission from the colonial governor prior to departure and to register their slaves upon arrival in France. Slaves were prohibited from staying longer than three years in France. A master who violated the provisions of the law would forfeit not only a 1,000-livre deposit (equivalent to the purchase price of a slave) but also the slave; the slave would be confiscated by the crown and resold in the colonies.

Some French courts accepted the king's new laws without objection, especially those of the Atlantic maritime provinces, with their strong interests in colonial commerce and the slave trade. But others—notably the Parlement of Paris, France's most important court—refused to register these laws, apparently because they used the term *slave*. The Paris judges, following the Freedom Principle, essentially held the laws to be counter to French traditions and the nation's unwritten constitution. Lower courts in the Paris jurisdiction refused to acknowledge a master's control over a slave and increasingly freed any slaves who protested their enslavement in court.

In 1759, the Parlement of Paris ruled on the case of Francisque, essentially supporting the Freedom Principle while simultaneously lending credibility to the notion of the racial inferiority of blacks. (See Document 5.) The king's 1777 law, known as the *Police des Noirs*, finally sidestepped the Freedom Principle by declaring that *all* non-whites (free or enslaved) who reached France must be quarantined in their port of arrival and shipped back to their colony of origin on the next available boat.

Over the eighteenth century, French metropolitan and colonial governments issued new legislation to establish and maintain racial hierarchy. For example, certain trades were forbidden to free people of color, including trading in gold and silver (1720), practicing medicine, surgery, and pharmacy (1764), and being employed as a clerk of court, notary, or bailiff (1765). Other laws sought to prohibit the accumulation of property through inheritance (1726). After the Seven Years' War (1756–1763), the French state took many new measures to prevent free people of color from flaunting any sign of elevated status. People with any African ancestry were prohibited from using the last names of whites. *Gens de couleur* (free people of color) were prohibited from assembling for feasts, even for weddings. In Saint-Domingue, former slaves and their descendants were pressed into mandatory military service that was not required of whites. In 1778, the French government prohibited marriages between whites and any person of color in the metropole. In both France and the colonies, new laws prohibited the use of the titles *Madame* and *Monsieur* by nonwhites in official documents (1781). And in 1779, a new law forbade *gens de couleur* from dressing or wearing their hair in the manner of whites. The character of these laws testifies not only to increasing restrictions on free people of color as a class, but also, implicitly, to the upward social mobility of *some* of these individuals and families.

Although the *Code Noir* forbade masters from having sex with their slaves, cases of white male masters having sex with black female slaves were not prosecuted by colonial governments, and mixed-race children were common.[2] Because a child's status followed that of the mother, these children would remain enslaved unless a master chose to free them. In the eighteenth century, French royal statutes made it difficult for masters who wanted to free their mixed-race children to do so. A new, quasi-free status known as *libre de savane* (free by the savanna) characterized slaves who were released from some or all of their labors but who were not recognized as free by the state.

By 1789, Saint-Domingue (Haiti, renowned then as the "Pearl of the Antilles") was the wealthiest colony in the world. Its eight thousand plantations produced sugar, coffee, cotton, indigo, and other products to support about two-fifths of France's overseas trade. Saint-Domingue also had the largest slave population in the Caribbean (450,000, or about 90 percent of the population). Half of these slaves had been born in Africa.[3] The free population of about 60,000 was almost equally divided between whites and *gens de couleur*. Whites ranged from soldiers, overseers, and merchants to members of the elite planter class (who owned huge plantations with hundreds of slaves). Free people of color included impoverished, sick, or elderly freedmen (some of whom were slaves who had been freed to spare the owner the expense of maintaining them), servants, and artisans. A small but vocal minority of these *gens de couleur* were wealthy plantation owners, the descendants of French colonists and African women, who had been educated in France, had inherited their father's land and slaves, and saw themselves as peers of their wealthy white counterparts.

Two revolutions—the French (begun in 1789) and the Haitian (begun in 1791)—changed both the legal frameworks and the practices of slavery in French colonies. The French Revolution's Declaration of the Rights of Man and Citizen (August 26, 1789) opened with the pronouncement "Men are born and remain free and equal." Early on, such republican ideology drew some whites and free people of color together, while the wealthiest planters tended to side with the monarchist parties. However, whites soon closed ranks and put down demands for racial equality. In August 1791, thousands of slaves in the northern plains of Saint-Domingue revolted, burning one thousand plantations and killing hundreds of whites in revenge for their treatment under slavery. Thousands of slaveholders fled the French colony

---

[2] Sex between black male slaves and white females was less common, and social and legal sanctions against it were strongly enforced.

[3] This was in marked contrast to the U.S. slave population at the outbreak of the U.S. Civil War in 1861. There the slave trade had been abolished for more than fifty years, and slaves were predominantly creole (native-born).

to North America and other parts of the Caribbean. The slave leaders, notably Jean-François and Georges Biassou, organized the rebels into armies; these prevailed against ill-seasoned French troops. On April 4, 1792, the Parisian National Assembly granted full citizenship to all free people in the colonies, regardless of color.

As the French and Haitian revolutions wore on, the Spanish and English saw the turmoil as an opportunity to pluck the pearl in France's imperial holdings, Saint-Domingue. When the French republican commissioner Sonthonax arrived there in 1793, he recognized the need for help from the rebel slaves, so he offered them legal freedom if they would fight on behalf of the republic. These soldiers—many under the command of the Spanish general Toussaint-Louverture, a brilliant strategist and former slave—were unimpressed, having already won practical freedom with machetes and guns. It was not until Sonthonax unilaterally abolished all slavery within the territory under his command that Louverture and his followers joined the side of the republic. In February 1794, the revolutionary government in Paris extended the abolition of slavery throughout the French empire. (See Document 8.) By 1799, Toussaint-Louverture was Saint-Domingue's undisputed leader. His colonial constitution of 1801 named him governor-for-life, with authority over all aspects of Saint-Dominguan society.

Meanwhile, in France, another general in the revolutionary army, Napoléon Bonaparte, rose to power by military coup. In 1802, Napoléon sent his brother-in-law, General Leclerc, with ten thousand soldiers to put down Toussaint and with secret instructions to restore slavery. Accompanying Leclerc were free mulatto officers, former planters who sought the return of their land and slaves. Leclerc tricked Toussaint, arrested him, and sent him to France, where the slave-turned-governor died in a cold mountain prison cell two years later. However, Leclerc's racist treatment of the mulatto officers pushed them to ally themselves with the former slaves.

On January 1, 1804, General Jean-Jacques Dessalines—a former ally of Leclerc—declared independence and named the new nation Haiti, based on the indigenous American Taino people's word meaning "mountainous, rugged." He confiscated the property of all whites and ordered them massacred (including those who had allied with the black army in the 1790s). Dessalines's deep distrust led to a falling out with the mulatto leadership; he was finally assassinated by their leader, Alexandre Pétion, in 1806. Thereafter, Haiti was divided between the mulatto president Pétion's republic, in the south, and the kingdom of Haiti, ruled by the black Henry Christophe, in the north. While Pétion's 1806 constitution (see Document 8) reflected a liberal republican ideology with regard to plantation laborers, subsequent legislation, like the Law of April 20, 1807, favored the rights of large landholders and sought to reorient agriculture toward an export economy, reinforcing the two-class system of landholders and workers.

France finally recognized independent Haiti in 1825, but only under the condition that the Haitian government pay "reparations" to France for loss of property—both land and slaves. Over the next fifty years, Haitians paid France nearly one hundred million livres, driving the country deeply into debt. Britain recognized Haiti in 1833, but the United States did not formally recognize the state until 1862, during the Civil War.

Napoléon's army successfully restored slavery to the remnants of the French empire, notably Guadeloupe and Martinique. Slavery persisted in these colonies until 1848, when it was abolished as part of a liberal revolution in the metropole.

The impact of the Haitian Revolution on the rest of the Atlantic World is complex and contradictory. Subsequent slave revolts and plots by free blacks—Venezuela (1795), Gabriel's Rebellion (Virginia, 1800), Louisiana (1811), Havana (1812), Charleston (1822), and Nat Turner's revolt (Virginia, 1831)—were at least partially inspired by the Haitian Revolution. More than a century after the initial slave revolt, the black American abolitionist and former U.S. ambassador to Haiti Frederick Douglass celebrated Haiti as "the only self-made Black Republic in the world." However, the horrors of the war—massacres, the burning of the capital city Cap-Français, 15,000 to 25,000 free and enslaved refugees—horrified whites on both sides of the Atlantic, prompting a backlash against the abolition movement. British antislavery activism subsided for more than a decade.

SLAVERY AND FREEDOM IN THE BRITISH ATLANTIC AND THE UNITED STATES

Like France, England originally had no laws regarding slavery. Though slavery had existed in England during the Roman and early medieval periods, by the time English settlers began to establish permanent colonies in North America and the Caribbean, slavery had died out as a legal category in English law. By the mid-seventeenth century, when African and Amerindian slaves were increasingly numerous in the English colonies, the colonists began to create local laws regarding slavery through their assemblies. As a result, the English empire—and later the United States—became a patchwork of independent and sometimes contradictory laws for slaves and citizens.

The English had no expectation or policy to rely on slave labor in America; like their French counterparts, early settlers indentured young men from their own country to cultivate the highly profitable cash crop of tobacco. Yet some English colonists purchased African or Amerindian slaves from the Spanish and Dutch, and with the introduction of sugar to Barbados in the 1630s, the slave plantation economy became established there. From Barbados, British slavery expanded into other tropical colonies—Suriname, Jamaica, Antigua, Montserrat, and Tobago—and into each of the original thirteen colonies on the mainland.

British North American slavery was not confined to the southern colonies. Rhode Island, the Hudson River Valley, and parts of New Jersey held significant slave populations; by the mid-eighteenth century, New York City had the second highest proportion of urban slaves among the thirteen colonies. Moreover, many northern colonies—notably Massachusetts, Rhode Island, Connecticut, and New York—were intimately connected to Caribbean slavery through money lending, slave trading, shipbuilding, sugar processing, and provisioning. Consequently, resistance to abolition was intense in many northern colonies, even those with low slave populations.

Even as slavery expanded in the British colonies of North America and the Caribbean, a new, very peculiar idea began to emerge on both sides of the Atlantic: the notion that slavery as an institution was wrong and ought to be abolished. To understand how strange abolitionism was, we must recognize that virtually every society in the world practiced slavery at some time in its history. While, generally speaking, nobody wanted to *be* a slave, the idea that slavery itself was fundamentally morally wrong was a novel one that emerged gradually but caught on rapidly in the late eighteenth and nineteenth centuries.

Historians have identified several roots of abolitionism. The first is slave resistance: A great many slaves were willing to work collectively to free themselves and their loved ones and, ultimately, to abolish slavery for everyone. Second, within Europe and dating back at least to the Middle Ages there was a popular antislavery tradition, especially in urban areas where escaped slaves and serfs enjoyed some protection under municipal laws and courts. Third, the radical egalitarianism of some evangelical religious movements, especially Quakerism, challenged hierarchies of all kinds, including slavery, as against God's will. Finally, some European elites began to question slavery as part of the eighteenth-century Enlightenment. These thinkers observed that slavery corrupted the character not only of the slaves, by encouraging them to appear weak, subservient, and ignorant, but also of the masters, by accustoming them to luxury and making them lazy and greedy. By the era of the American Revolution, the notion that slavery was wrong and would ultimately have to be abolished was widespread—though not universal—in both the Americas and northern Europe.

In England, France, and certain parts of North America (especially Pennsylvania and Massachusetts), citizens organized antislavery societies. These voluntary groups gave public lectures, published pamphlets, books, and letters, and looked for ways to publicize the horrible wrong of slavery. One group in London settled upon a particularly interesting strategy: They would try to get the English Court of King's Bench to rule that slavery was illegal in England. Their efforts resulted in the landmark *Somerset* decision of 1772. (See Document 10.) The *Somerset* case established that slaves could not be held against their will in England; for all intents and purposes, it abolished slavery in England. After the United States achieved independence, many legal decisions there cited *Somerset* as a precedent, giving momentum and a particularly legalistic trajectory to the U.S. antislavery movement.

Following the *Somerset* decision, abolitionist sentiment spread rapidly in England, while Britain's West Indian colonies—including the Bahamas, Barbados, British Honduras (Belize), Bermuda, Dominica, Grenada, Jamaica, the Leeward Islands, and Trinidad and Tobago—continued to import thousands of slaves from Africa every year. The most fervent antislavery proponents demanded immediate and complete abolition, while more cautious supporters argued for gradual emancipation, beginning with the termination of the slave trade. However, the French and Haitian revolutions of the 1790s and early 1800s provoked a conservative reaction in England, interrupting the abolitionists' efforts. Thirty-five years would pass between the *Somerset* decision and the legal proclamation abolishing the British slave trade (1807). Between 1807 and 1860, British diplomats negotiated treaties banning the slave trade with more than 120 countries, even as Britain extended its empire throughout Africa, the Middle East, and Asia.

The United States outlawed the transatlantic slave trade in 1807, effective the next year. The U.S. and British paths toward abolition diverged thereafter. Though many English antislavery activists assumed that colonial slavery would slowly die out, British West Indian planters were highly motivated to retain their labor supply and even resisted Parliament's attempts to improve slaves' living and working conditions. In the Caribbean colonies and in Parliament, evangelical missionaries worked with slaves to agitate for general emancipation. British Caribbean slaves challenged their enslavement in three important rebellions: Barbados in 1816, Demerara in 1823, and Jamaica in 1831. (There were two other major slave insurrections in 1831: in French Martinique and Nat Turner's revolt in Virginia.) Frustrated with the lack of progress and planter opposition, British abolitionists increasingly demanded immediate, universal, and unconditional emancipation.

Finally, in 1833 Parliament passed a twenty-four-page act that would abolish slavery as of August 1, 1834. This decisive legislative act was possible in part because of the centralized authority of the British Parliament. The decentralized power of individual states and the centrality of slavery to the U.S. economy made immediate action much more difficult in the United States. Like the work regulations instituted immediately after emancipation in Saint-Domingue and Haiti, the British emancipation act created an "apprenticeship" system, designed to last until 1840. Under this system, the newly emancipated freedmen in British colonies were forced to continue working three-quarters of the time for their former masters; the remainder of their time was to be spent raising food on their own garden plots for self-support. The act arranged to compensate masters for their loss of property and to pay wages to these free laborers, which created an enormous financial obligation—equivalent to half of England's national budget. This apprenticeship system finally broke down in 1838, at which time slavery can truly be said to have been abolished in the British West Indies.

It is worth pausing a moment to ask why the world's biggest slave trader would abolish an institution that was clearly a major and growing source of wealth. Historians have debated these questions (and their premises) for more than half a century now. Some, following historian Eric Williams, argue that American slavery generated enormous wealth for England and the United States, even financing the great industrial revolution. Yet after the American Revolutionary War, slave economies declined in profitability and importance to England, thus lessening the English commitment to slavery. Other historians, such as Roger Anstey, have pointed to the great religious revival of the late eighteenth and early nineteenth centuries, arguing that this new moralism motivated American and British abolitionists. David Brion Davis connects these religious motivations to the political ferment of the Age of Revolution, in which Americans, British, and French celebrated the rights of man and the spread of democratic ideals. Seymour Drescher has pointed out that England's political culture of representative democracy made common men and women feel that their voices mattered, so thousands signed petitions, attended rallies, and pressured the government to end the slave trade and slavery itself. More recently, Robin Blackburn has expanded the circle of analysis to show how abolition came about in a series of economic and political crises that extended beyond the North Atlantic societies of England, France, and the United States to encompass the independence movements of Spanish America and Brazil. Rebecca Scott and others are working to understand how slaves themselves used a range of tactics—from collective political organization to military action to legal cases—to claim the rights of humanity and citizenship in Cuba and other parts of the Atlantic World. In sum, many factors contributed to abolitionist beliefs, but it was only through generations of political activism and, in some cases, bloodshed, that slavery finally came to be abolished throughout Europe and the Americas.

Meanwhile, the abolition movement in the United States began to gain steam with propaganda campaigns and vast petition drives against the internal slave trade. Abolitionists mobilized against the introduction of slavery to the new publicly owned federal territories of the expanding American West. They seized upon the *Amistad* case to publicize the injustices of slavery. African slaves, smuggled illegally from Sierre Leone to Cuba, revolted aboard the ship, *La Amistad*, in 1839 and finally came ashore on Long Island, New York. It took three years and dedicated efforts by the captives, lawyers, linguists, missionaries, and activists, including former president John Quincy Adams, to persuade the Supreme Court to release the survivors, most of whom returned to their African homeland. Some historians believe that the *Amistad* case prompted Chief Justice Roger Taney's Court to issue the infamous *Dred Scott* decision almost two decades later, in 1857. That decision held that, by virtue of being black, Scott—a slave who had accompanied his master from Virginia, a slave state, into the free state of Illinois—had no standing to bring suit in a court of law. The Supreme Court ruled against Scott's freedom. Three years later, the United States erupted into civil war.

Racism—the idea that people classified as "white" were innately superior to others and therefore deserved privileges that would be denied to various classes of nonwhites—had intensified in the United States in the 1830s, largely as a response to abolitionism, gaining widespread acceptance in both the North and the South, influencing both slaveholders and many white abolitionists. Racism did not merely circulate as chauvinism or prejudice, but was codified into law, thus throwing the considerable apparatus of the state (police, courts, penal system) behind the stratification of U.S. society. (See Document 15.) While not all whites endorsed racism, the few who actively worked against the system of inequality joined black Americans in an uphill battle to guarantee the privileges of American citizenship to all Americans.

The United States Civil War (1861–1865) prompted the remaining American slaveholding powers, especially Cuba and Brazil, to consider the price of resisting emancipation. Though Abraham Lincoln's Emancipation Proclamation (January 1, 1863) freed slaves only in states that had seceded from the Union, it was one of the few cases in which slaveholders did not receive "reparations" in the form of monetary compensation or the free labor of former slaves.

The fate of the freedmen in the postemancipation period was mixed. The Fourteenth Amendment to the U.S. Constitution (1868) should have ensured equal status to all former slaves (see Document 19), but many legislatures and courts, particularly in the South, enacted and enforced laws that bound large numbers of blacks into subservient agricultural labor and reinforced their second-class status until the middle of the twentieth century. (See Document 21.)

SLAVERY AND FREEDOM
IN THE SPANISH ATLANTIC

Slavery never totally disappeared in the Spanish kingdoms of Aragon and Castile during the Middle Ages, though the relatively few slaves of this period were employed almost exclusively as servants. Starting in the fourteenth century, Muslim traders brought slaves from sub-Saharan Africa to Spain, where both Christians and Muslims considered them barbarians and infidels.

From 1492 until 1886, some 1.5 million enslaved Africans were brought to the Spanish colonies of America. Early on, most agricultural labor in the Spanish colonies was performed by indigenous people under a tributary system known as *encomienda*. In practice, however, working conditions and Spanish imperial rule were as brutal as chattel slavery for many native peoples. African slaves, by contrast, often performed skilled trades like blacksmithing or herding cattle and therefore occupied a somewhat higher social rank than native peoples. (See Document 23.)

The Spanish brought medieval Castilian law to Spanish America. It is difficult to establish to what extent colonists applied the 1265 legal code, *Las Siete Partidas*, in the New World, but at least some of its provisions regulated the existence of slaves as well as their descendants. (See Document 22.) Consistent with Roman jurisprudence, Spanish law considered slavery to be contrary to nature and held liberty as the natural state of man. The law restricted slaveowners' power; for example, the type and intensity of punishment were limited, and an owner who raped or beat a slave severely could be forced to sell the slave. Spanish law also favored emancipation. As a result, from the beginning of the African presence on Spanish lands in America, many slaves were freed, primarily through payment of their value.

Coartación, or self-purchase—a mechanism that allowed slaves to pay for their freedom, either in one lump payment or by installments—was a special characteristic of Spanish slave law, though also found in some regions of Brazil. Since the end of the eighteenth century—and perhaps much earlier—colonists accepted and affirmed the basic principles underwriting *coartación*: that slaves who paid their value had the right to manumission; that after receiving this value, the owner had the obligation to provide a letter of manumission; that *coartación* was a personal right (it did not pass from mother to daughter, for example); and that, after being set, the price of a slave could not be changed (for example, an owner could not increase the price by alleging that he had taught the slave a trade). Documents from *coartación* proceedings show that the relationships between slaveowners and slaves involved negotiation and tensions and the establishment of rights and duties; slaves did not simply submit to the will of the slaveowner. (See Documents 25 and 26.)

Coartación, the most common way for Africans and their descendants to become free, led to the emergence of a large population of freeborn and freed people of African descent in Spanish America. By the end of the eighteenth century, in various regions of South America including Peru and Ecuador, there were almost as many free Afro-descendants as there were slaves.

Although the Spanish empire comprised the largest territory of the Americas, and Spain maintained vestiges of its American colonial empire longer than other European imperial powers, the number of slaves employed for local labor was small in the Spanish colonies compared to the French, English, and Portuguese colonies. Aside from a few plantation areas concentrated in Peru and Venezuela, landowners did not invest their wealth in slaves, nor did they typically use slaves for heavy manual labor. Only 12 percent of all Africans brought to the New World were taken to Spanish America. The majority of these originated in the Portuguese African colonies of Cape Verde, São Tomé, Angola, and Mozambique. Moreover, Spanish America contained a great diversity of forms of slavery. In regions like Mexico and Central America, the role of slave labor was marginal. Spanish use of slave labor peaked in Venezuela and Peru in the sixteenth through eighteenth centuries, though even then the production of cocoa, sugar, tobacco, and indigo that reached Spain was not even sufficient to satisfy metropolitan desires; there was no surplus available for the world market.

In the second half of the eighteenth century, however, colonists and the crown began to try to enhance the profitability of the Spanish colonies in the Caribbean to make them as productive as those of England and France. The expulsion of Jesuits from the Spanish empire in 1767 and the confiscation of their goods—which included numerous slaves—transformed the crown into the largest slaveowner in Spanish America. Facing competition with the newly independent United States of America and the possibility of reaping high profits through the introduction of a plantation economy, the Spanish crown expanded its importation of Africans with the establishment of free trade in 1778 and with the law of free traffic in 1789. Although Cuba is not the only place where plantation agriculture played a central role in Spanish America, it provides a very interesting case study.

In contrast to continental Spanish America, which relied heavily on indigenous workers, African slaves became the primary labor force in Cuba starting in the mid-sixteenth century. Some slaves lived near the main cities, where they could work through a "hiring-out system," paying a fixed daily amount to their owners. However, most lived in small rural production units of about fifteen slaves. Slaves' varied economic functions enabled many to accumulate sufficient wealth to purchase their freedom. By 1792, free people of color accounted for 20 percent of the total population. Only when Cubans shifted from tobacco to sugar cultivation at the end of the eighteenth century did the number of slaves in the *haciendas* begin to increase, accompanied by a rise in the slave trade.

The social and legal practices that existed in Cuba until the end of the eighteenth century, which were very similar to other areas of Spanish America, changed drastically with the expansion of the plantation economy and its overwhelming impact on racial relations. Though the slave population rose from 84,590 in 1792 to 399,872 in 1861, slaves remained only about one-third of Cuba's total population, due to simultaneous immigration of whites and natural reproduction of the free population. The new sugar barons now had sufficient power to impose their rigorous labor discipline, pushing aside the state's efforts to regulate relations with slaves. When, for example, the Spanish crown published the *Instrucción sobre Educación, Trato y Ocupación de los Esclavos* in 1789 (see Document 24), owners mobilized to prevent it from being put into practice, claiming that the legislation would bring an end to discipline and the owners' authority over their slaves. At the same time, they managed to overturn some centuries-old customs, such as acceptance of interracial marriages, which, after 1805, required special permission from local authorities. The old social and legal practices did not disappear immediately, however, partly because plantations were not predominant throughout the entire island. They were almost nonexistent, for example, in the eastern part of Cuba, where free Africans and Afro-descendants represented almost one-third of the total population. The free nonwhite community continued to grow through natural reproduction and self-purchase, especially in urban areas.

In 1817, the Spanish crown signed a treaty with England for the abolition of the slave trade, which should have entered into force in 1820. Ironically, however, the Spanish trade grew *more* rapidly after the threat of interruption. So many slaves came to Cuba from Africa and the other Spanish colonies that by 1841 they constituted 41 percent of the Cuban population. In 1845, British pressure finally forced Spain to restrict the traffic in slaves.

To control so much labor, Cuba and Puerto Rico adopted new legislation similar to other Atlantic slave codes, from the French *Code Noir* to the eighteenth-century codes of Santo Domingo (1768), Louisiana (1769), Hispaniola (1784) (see Document 24), and the American South. A series of slave revolts in Puerto Rico (1821–1825) and Cuba (1840s), along with persistent pressures by growing rural and urban *quilombos* (maroon communities), prompted authorities to issue additional laws to regulate the relations between slaves and owners and to define the obligations of each.

The wars of independence of the nineteenth century marked the final phase of slavery in Spanish American mainland colonies. Antislavery views spread rapidly during this time. (See Document 27.) Simón Bolívar used the call for abolition as a recruitment tool and, not surprisingly, drew many former slaves into his army. Chile abolished slavery in 1823, Mexico in 1829, while the practice dwindled in Bolivia and Central America.

Despite the widespread condemnation of slavery, the institution persisted in some newly independent republics, such as Venezuela, Colombia, and Peru. (See Document 28.) Slavery lingered on the outskirts of cities like Lima, Caracas, and Buenos Aires, where slaves were primarily artisans, field workers, construction workers, or domestic workers. At the middle of the nineteenth century, there were still about 225,000 slaves in continental Spanish America. Yet within a decade, slavery was abolished on the Spanish American mainland, ending with Peru and Venezuela in 1854.

By contrast, in 1868, Cuba's expanding sugar production had reached the impressive level of 720,250 metric tons—more than 40 percent of total global production. (See Document 29.) This same year marked the beginning of a long war for Cuban independence, which ended in 1898 after the United States invaded the island. One year after the war began, independence leaders decreed the end of Cuban slavery and issued regulations governing former slaves, which required each freedman to have a patron, usually the former master. But as the war continued, thousands of Cubans remained enslaved in areas loyal to Spain.

The war of independence in Cuba provoked conflicting reactions in Spain. On one hand, the Spanish did not want to lose the support of the remaining loyalist plantation owners, nor did they want a decrease in sugar production, so they opposed the abolition of slavery. At the same time, they recognized the growing strength of the abolitionist movement on the island and in Spain and wanted to draw Afro-Cubans, as well as landowners favorable to emancipation, away from the independence movement, so they supported some abolitionist policies.

In 1872, to try to overcome this ambiguity, Spain promulgated a gradual emancipation policy, known as the Moret Law. Like other Atlantic "free womb" laws—for example, Pennsylvania (1780), Chile (1811), Peru (1821), and Brazil (1871)—the Moret Law established that all children born after a certain date would be free. Children born to slave parents would remain under the tutelage of their mother's owners until the age of eighteen to provide for "assimilation to the culture and civilization of Spain."

Under the Moret Law, the total number of slaves in Cuba dropped from around 300,000 to fewer than 200,000 in 1877. The law had little effect on those of working age, however, freeing mostly children and the elderly. New labor strategies, meanwhile, led to a period of economic prosperity, even while the war for independence wore on. In the regions affected by the war, many plantations were destroyed, which led to the freeing of many slaves; at the same time, in other regions not affected by the war, sugar production prospered and slavery persisted. Where slavery continued, owners began diversifying their labor force, renting others' slaves, contracting Asian immigrants, and hiring free white, black, and mulatto workers. Landowners hoped to replace slave labor gradually, keeping pace with the decline of the slave population. That, however, was not what happened. The proliferation of antislavery ideas in Spain, the duration of the war and the destruction of plantations, the resulting liberation of slaves, and the pressures of the slaves themselves brought about a more immediate end to slavery.

Following the radical overthrow of the Spanish monarchy in 1873, the new Spanish Republic immediately proclaimed the liberation of all slaves in Puerto Rico. Cuba was more problematic because of the strong slaveholding class. In 1879, Spanish leaders appointed Cuban slaveowners and others to a commission to study slavery in Cuba. Although everyone recognized the need for eventual abolition—if only because of the threat of slave insurrection—both the governor general and the slaveowners emphasized the risks of immediate abolition. The commission proposed an arrangement whereby slavery would be replaced temporarily with a *patronato* system, similar to the way the British abolition was followed by a term of apprenticeship. The resulting *Patronato* law of 1880 (Document 33) brought about the end of slavery in Cuba and Spanish America in 1886.

Although Africans and their descendants made up the majority of slaves in Spanish America, legislation following abolition was not explicitly racist. There were, for example, no formal mechanisms preventing nonwhites from exercising their citizenship, as there were in the United States. This resulted from former slaves' soldiering in the Latin American wars of independence and their demands for full citizenship in the new nations. This does not mean, however, that Hispanic American societies had not incorporated the racist practices that predominated during the centuries of slave labor. Even today, the quality of life and the opportunities for social advancement of Afro-descendants in Spanish America are still far inferior to those of the population considered "white."

SLAVERY AND FREEDOM IN THE PORTUGUESE ATLANTIC AND BRAZIL

In the fifteenth century, the Portuguese crown sought to unify and regularize the varying municipal, Roman, and canonical laws in the general legal codes known as *Ordenações*. The *Ordenações Afonsinas*, enacted during the reign of King Afonso V (1438–1481), set out the civil, taxation, administrative, military, and penal laws. This compilation was revised twice: in 1521, during the reign of King Manuel (the *Ordenações Manuelinas*), and in 1603, during the reign of King Philip II, when they were renamed *Ordenações Filipinas*. (See Document 34.) The *Ordenações Filipinas* remained in force, with some modifications, until 1867 in Portugal, when the Civil Code was promulgated in that country, and until 1917 in Brazil, when it was replaced by the Civil Code.

The *Ordenações Filipinas* mention slaves and the slave regime frequently. Throughout the entire medieval period, Portugal maintained close contact with the Islamic societies of the Mediterranean, which trafficked in African slaves and also continued to enslave individuals, especially those captured in battles against the Moors (Muslim inhabitants of the Iberian Peninsula).

At the height of its power, the Portuguese Empire included settlements as dispersed as São Tomé and Príncipe, Madeira, Angola, and Mozambique in Africa; Goa in India; Macao near China; and of course Brazil. A unified legal code governed this vast empire. Although many of its provisions fell into disuse over the centuries and were gradually replaced by more modern legislation, the basic principles underlying the *Ordenações Filipinas* regulated relations between masters and slaves up until at least the 1820s, when Brazil declared independence from Portugal. After this, even with the gradual replacement of Portuguese colonial legislation by new laws, many of the preexisting basic rules covering slavery continued in force in Brazilian society until 1888, when the regime of slave labor was finally abolished.

Portuguese slave law, like Spain's, took from Roman law the conception of slavery as being contrary to the natural state of man. It was assumed that legislation should, in general, favor human liberty. As in Spanish America, there were limits to the power of masters over their slaves. A large number of individual slaves were emancipated, in part because there were no legal restrictions on this practice.

There were three principal ways by which masters freed their slaves in Brazil: by a letter of liberty (or letter of manumission), by will and testament, or at the "baptismal font" (in the act of baptism). Most of the beneficiaries of freedom through baptism were children. In the case of emancipation declared in wills, it was common for slaves to be *conditionally* manumitted: They would need to work a given number of years, or until one of the heirs of their master died, in order to gain their freedom. There were also the cases of *coartação* (self-purchase), similar to the Spanish American practice of *coartación*, when slaves paid the price of their liberty in installments. (See Document 36.) Less common in Brazil than in its Spanish American neighbors, the practice of *coartação* was widespread in the province of Minas Gerais, where mining activity and the possibility of finding and secreting very valuable precious stones contributed to slaves' ability to purchase their own freedom. (See Document 35.) Theoretically, masters could revoke manumission on the grounds of ingratitude if the freed slave did not show sufficient respect and loyalty to the former master. Such revocation occurred primarily during the colonial period, fell into disuse over the nineteenth century, and was practically nonexistent from the 1860s onward.

Little is known about how many slaves achieved emancipation in Brazil during the colonial period (until 1822). We do know that the majority of these were women, and most were born in Brazil. They generally lived in cities; those who lived in rural areas performed domestic functions. (See Documents 36 and 38.) As more of these women became free, they, in turn, gave birth to new generations of free Afro-descendants. This led to an ever-increasing free black urban population in Brazil.

At least 40 percent of the Africans brought to the Americas throughout the entire period of the transatlantic slave trade ended up in Brazil. Although the exact number is unknown, at least four million Africans came to Brazil, not counting those who died on the way (the mortality rate ranged from 15 to 25 percent). This situation meant that slaves born in Africa (as opposed to creole slaves) made up a significant portion of the Brazilian population. There were places where, because of the importance of the sugarcane economy, around 65 percent of the slave population was African-born.

This does not mean that slave labor was organized in the same way throughout Brazil. On the contrary, Portuguese America was home to extremely diverse forms of slavery. There were agro-exporting areas, such as the Brazilian northeast in the seventeenth century; mining areas, such as Minas Gerais in the eighteenth century; and urban areas, such as the cities of Salvador, Recife, and Rio de Janeiro. The characteristics and roles of the slave labor regime varied with the dynamics of the regional economy. When slavery was in decline in Pernambuco and Bahia in the nineteenth century, for example, it flourished in the region of the Paraíba River Valley (around São Paulo and Rio de Janeiro) with the expansion of coffee cultivation.

The nineteenth century was the most controversial period in the history of Brazilian slavery. Following Brazil's independence from Portugal, proclaimed in 1822, some liberal politicians began to challenge the slave labor regime. (See Document 40.) During the struggle for independence, slaves were encouraged to enlist in the armed forces, with the promise of being freed when the conflict was over; this strengthened their sense of entitlement to freedom and citizenship. Meanwhile, an estimated 1.5 million slaves entered the country in the first half of the century due to the strength of the coffee economy. The government issued the first laws restricting the slave trade in 1831. This first slave trade ban was poorly enforced, so England pressured the Brazilian government, even invading Brazilian maritime territory in search of slave smugglers. Brazil finally effectively abolished the transatlantic slave trade in 1850. (See Document 41.)

The elimination of the slave trade unleashed profound changes in demographic, political, social, and economic structures in Brazil. The most important impact was an increase in the internal Brazilian slave trade, with massive sales of slaves from the provinces of the northeast, in economic decline, to the central southern region, in the midst of the coffee boom. The end of the Atlantic slave trade also led to a rapid rise in the price of slaves, which in turn led to a great concentration of slave ownership. Until 1850, even freed slaves and poor laborers could afford to buy a slave, but after that point slaves became too expensive for anyone except large landowners involved in export agriculture.

The end of the Atlantic slave trade and the high concentration of slave ownership dealt a death blow to the free population's commitment to slave labor in Brazil. Although it would take thirty-eight years from the end of slave trade until the abolition of slavery in Brazil, it can be argued that the legitimacy of the slave labor regime had been severely weakened in 1850.

The next decisive legal blow to Brazilian slavery came in 1871 with the Free Womb Law. (See Documents 43 and 44.) As the name suggests, all children born after the law's passage would be free. However, the children of slaves would remain the responsibility of their masters until the age of eight or twenty-one; when masters chose the younger age, they would receive compensation from the government. To this end, the law created an Emancipation Fund to liberate an annual quota of slaves, and it imposed a head tax on slaves (to be paid by slaveowners). Significantly, the law recognized the right of the slave to possess savings, whether through donations, legacy, or inheritance or obtained "by consent of the master" from their labor and economy. Slaves could do what they wished with this money, including purchase their freedom, and their masters could not stop them. (See Document 45.) The Free Womb Law thus had a tremendous impact on Brazilian society, from establishing a range of slaves' rights to setting limits on the master's authority.

Eventually, with the end of the U.S. Civil War (1865) and the liberation of Cuba's slaves (1886), Brazil became isolated as the only slave nation in the Americas. On May 3, 1888, the abolition-minded Princess Isabel—the daughter of Dom Pedro II, who was not in the country at the time—sanctioned the Áurea Law, which ended slavery in Brazil with no conditions or compensation to the slaveowners. (See Document 46.) After emancipation, despite a lack of explicitly racist Brazilian legislation, a new framework of racial inequalities emerged in the absence of policies for social integration of freed slaves. This helps explain the persistent social inequalities between those considered "white" and those considered "black" in Brazil.

THE MEANING OF FREEDOM

When we look at the history of slavery, freedom, and the law in the Atlantic World comparatively, setting different empires and local contexts side by side, several important themes emerge. These include contrasting imperial legal traditions regarding slavery; the impact of gender on slaves, especially as they sought free status; the different meanings of freedom (marronage, the independence of fugitive slaves; manumission; general emancipation; citizenship); and the establishment of institutional forms of racism.

We can make a clear distinction between, on the one hand, the Spanish and Portuguese legal traditions of the South Atlantic and, on the other, the French and English traditions of the North Atlantic. Both the Spanish and the Portuguese had unified legal codes, based in Roman law, that both regulated slavery and favored individual manumission. Since Islamic and medieval times, the Spanish and Portuguese (sometimes called "Iberians") maintained a small minority— but a real presence—of slaves within their populations. Consequently, a body of slave law persisted to regulate slaves as property and as people. These laws carried into the Spanish and Portuguese colonial settlements in Africa and the Americas. By contrast, the French and English had no positive law regarding slavery. The French government recognized a principle that gave slaves their freedom as soon as they set foot on French soil in Europe. At first, the English wavered on the question of whether Christian baptism would confer freedom on a slave. However, as slavery became integral to the British and French colonies, each developed local colonial traditions—and eventually laws—to regulate slaves and their masters differently from the laws that applied to the metropoles.

One of the first historians to become interested in the contrast between northern and southern Atlantic cultures regarding race and slavery was Frank Tannenbaum. Tannenbaum's primary interest was in race relations; in his classic 1947 study, *Slave and Citizen*, he noted that Brazilians, in particular, were relatively open to men of mixed race acting in politics, high culture, and business, while in the United States the so-called one-drop rule excluded people of mixed African and European ancestry from elite positions. Tannenbaum traced these traditions back to Latin America's higher rates of manumission. He argued that Latin Americans were more likely to free their slaves than British colonists because of the influence of Catholicism and Roman law, which recognized the inherent humanity of slaves.

Many historians have since criticized both Tannenbaum's assumptions and his conclusions, offering a wide range of explanations for variations in rates of manumission. For example, societies or locations with a relatively small number of slaves have tended to favor manumission; when plantation slavery came to dominate a region, many governments, regardless of religious or legal traditions, instituted taxes and other policies that made it difficult for masters to manumit their slaves for fear of nonwhites outnumbering the white ruling elite. Other historians point to the custom of self-purchase, where a slave could accumulate enough money through day labor, trade, or other means to buy his or her own freedom (*coartación* or *coartação*). This occurred most frequently in cities and towns, where slaves could participate in a cash economy, and in gold-mining regions, where they could accumulate a portion of their findings to buy their freedom.

Finally, there are interesting gender dimensions to manumission. In general, masters manumitted women and children more frequently than adult male slaves; many of those freed may have been the masters' concubines and children, but a great many also earned their freedom through trade and self-purchase. Widespread use of plantation slave labor came late to Latin America, and when it did, so did legal bars to manumission.

It would be a mistake to see freedom primarily as something that was "handed down" by colonial or European elites to slaves. Slaves sought, negotiated for, and demanded their freedom both individually and collectively, as can be seen in these documents. Maroons escaped their enslavement and engaged in guerrilla warfare. Enslaved women publicly shamed their masters for sexual abuse and breach of contract in lawsuits for freedom. Miners petitioned collectively to form mutual aid societies to purchase one another's freedom. Some slaves joined the armies of both revolutionary and imperial governments in exchange for promises of freedom. Others who escaped, for example via the Underground Railroad, worked tirelessly to abolish slavery by legislative act. They had allies in the form of ministers, lawyers, petition signers, politicians, editors, and soldiers. Without the initiative and actions of slaves and former slaves, it seems unlikely that slavery could have been undone.

The kind of freedom that was gained by individual slaves—whether through manumission, escape, or individual court cases—should be distinguished from general emancipation, where a state or national government abolished slavery throughout its territory. Many historians believe that individualized freedom paradoxically *reinforced* the institution of slavery as a whole because it functioned as a kind of safety valve. If slaves could see that a few among them could gain their freedom (especially through compliance with the master's demands), then perhaps they would be more likely to behave well in hopes that they, too, would someday be freed. Indeed, some slave societies reinforced this contradiction by granting freedom to slaves who helped capture runaways or who fought in maroon wars. This is very different from the abolitionists' collective action to try to emancipate an entire class of people.

We can further distinguish between military action by slaves and their supporters (in slave revolts or the Haitian Revolution) to escape oppression and fight against the master class, and abolitionists' efforts to reform the law and emancipate slaves. While many abolitionists had moral misgivings about slavery, few were committed to a radical vision of complete egalitarianism. Consequently, after general emancipation, many European powers and their colonial counterparts moved quickly to find ways to coerce the vast agricultural labor force to continue producing profitable export goods. These goods—sugar, cotton, tobacco, cocoa—would feed the rapidly growing consumer class of the late eighteenth and nineteenth centuries.

It seems ironic that at precisely the same time that people in the European Atlantic empires were challenging the injustice of slavery, many were inventing and asserting the privileges of race. The late eighteenth and nineteenth centuries witnessed the emergence and hegemony of a racial regime that reverberated throughout the Americas. French and U.S. legal codes, in particular, codified whiteness as a category with specific rights, so that even while many whites came to believe that slavery was wrong, some of the same people insisted on the inferiority of blacks and other nonwhites. In Spanish and Portuguese America, racism was less formally institutionalized (for example, with differential voting rights based on race), but informal hierarchies (such as control of literacy and landownership) reinforced the powers of Euro-descendants over the descendants of colonized Amerindians or forced migrant laborers from Africa.

In the nineteenth century, most abolition policies forced slaves to compensate their owners for loss of property. For example, the governments of France and Haiti forced former slaves and their descendants to pay "reparations" for their liberation (laying the groundwork for Haiti's poverty today). Similarly, the gradualist "free womb" policies adopted in many northern U.S. states and in Latin America compensated masters by requiring former slaves to work without wages for a number of years beyond childhood. In the late twentieth century, some African Americans organized a reparations movement, turning the nineteenth-century idea on its head. Leaders of this movement argue that the descendants of slaves should be compensated since their ancestors' labor was unfairly stolen from them by force. Moreover, in the wake of emancipation, racial discrimination (some of it enforced by legislation and judicial decisions) has perpetuated political, social, and economic inequalities to the present day. This book's epilogue describes a legal case that suggests that reparations for slaves is not necessarily a new idea. It provides us with the fascinating and provocative story of an Afro-Cuban woman, Andrea Quesada, who, in the first years of the twentieth century, determined to use the law to compensate herself and other former slaves for their labor prior to abolition in 1886.

Despite the legal abolition of slavery in the nineteenth century, slavery remains a problem in today's world. Women and children remain especially vulnerable to human trafficking, from the production of cocoa in West Africa to forced prostitution in Europe, Asia, and other parts of the world. It is worthwhile to ponder how coercive labor practices, migration and citizenship regulation, penal systems, and global capitalism compare and contrast to forms of slavery and freedom of the past. Today nongovernmental organizations (NGOs) from the United Nations to Anti-Slavery and Free the Slaves are working to secure basic human rights for all people.

By bringing together documents from the major imperial enterprises of the late eighteenth and nineteenth centuries, we invite you to take part in the discovery and debate of the meanings of freedom in the modern Atlantic. This area of research is so new that it is possible that you and your classmates will have insights and make new connections that professional historians have not yet imagined. In so doing, you will become part of a new generation of historical scholars who can radically reshape our understanding of the world.

PART TWO

The Documents

1

The French Atlantic
and the Haitian Revolution

1

FRENCH CROWN

The Code Noir

1685

The 1685 Code Noir *(Black Code) was the first integrated slave code written specifically for the Americas. It served as a model for later slave legislation under Dutch and Spanish regimes. The* Code Noir *reflected the tendency toward increasing bureaucratization and systemization under Louis XIV. Derived from customary practices already developed in the colonies since the 1630s, the* Code Noir *was a collaborative effort by colonial officials and Catholic missionaries, modified by input from royal officials in Versailles.*

Edict of the King concerning the Enforcement of Order in the Islands of America, Versailles, March 1685

[The first eight articles allowed only the Catholic religion to be practiced in the French slave colonies. They expelled all Jews, required the Catholic baptism of all slaves, prohibited Protestants from practicing their religion

---

"Code Noir, touchant la police des isles de l'Amérique," Versailles, March 1685, in François-André Isambert, *Recueil général des anciennes lois françaises depuis l'an 420 jusqu'à la révolution de 1789* (Paris, 1830). Translated by Sue Peabody.

in public or teaching it to slaves, kept Sunday a day of rest by forbidding masters to make their slaves work and prohibiting the slave markets on Sunday, and outlawed non-Catholic marriages.]

9. Free men who sire one or more children with slaves out of wedlock, together with the masters who permitted this, will each be condemned to a fine of two thousand pounds of sugar. And if they are the masters of the slave by whom they have had the said children, we wish that, in addition to the fine, they be deprived of the slave and the children, and that she and they be confiscated for the profit of the [royal] hospital, without ever being manumitted. Nevertheless we do not intend for the present article to be enforced if the man was not married to another person during his concubinage with his slave, and if he marries the said slave according to the church's formalities. She, then, by this means will be manumitted and the children rendered free and legitimate.

[Articles 10–11 regulated marriage in the French slave colonies. The law required parental consent for free people to marry but only a master's consent for slaves. Masters could not force slaves to marry against their will.]

12. Children who are born of a marriage between slaves will be slaves and will belong to the master of the women slaves, and not to those of their husbands, if the husband and the wife have different masters.

13. We wish that if a slave husband has married a free woman, the children, both male and female, follow the condition of their mother and be free like her, in spite of the servitude of their father; and that if the father is free and the mother is enslaved, the children will likewise be slaves.

[Articles 14–18 established lawful burial practices for slaves, forbade slaves from carrying weapons (unless the master had permitted the slave to go hunting), prohibited large slave gatherings for marriages or other purposes, and set limits on slaves' ability to engage in commerce. For example, they could not sell sugar under any circumstances, presumably to prevent them from stealing from their masters.]

19. We also forbid them from displaying for sale at the market or from carrying to private houses for sale any kind of commodity—

even fruits, vegetables, firewood, grasses for feeding animals, and their crafts—without express permission of their masters. . . .

[Articles 20–21 established police to monitor slaves' compliance with Article 19 and allowed any free colonist to confiscate any of the mentioned items from slaves and to arrest the slave unless the slave had the master's written permission to engage in local markets. Articles 22–25 attempted to prevent masters from abusing their slaves by insisting on minimum rations of food and clothing, forbidding the distribution of rum in lieu of staple foods, and forbidding masters from making slaves raise their own food in garden plots. This last provision was not enforced.]

26. Slaves who are not fed, clothed, and supported by their masters according to what we have ordered by these articles will notify our attorney of this and give him their statements. Based on this, and even as a matter of course if the information comes to him from elsewhere, the king's attorney general will prosecute the masters without cost. We want [these articles] to be observed for the crimes and barbarous and inhumane treatments of masters towards their slaves.

27. Slaves who are infirm by age, sickness, or otherwise . . . will be fed and maintained by their masters. And in the case when they are abandoned, the slaves will be awarded to the hospital, to which the masters will be required to pay sixpence per day, for the nourishment and maintenance of each slave.

28. We declare that slaves can own nothing that does not belong to their masters. And everything that comes to them—by their own industry, by the generosity of others, or otherwise—. . . be acquired in full property to their masters, without the slaves' children, their fathers and mothers, their relatives or any others, being able to claim anything of it by inheritance, donations inter vivos, or because of death. We declare such dispositions null, together with any promises and obligations that they have made, as being made by people incapable of disposing and contracting on their own initiative.

29. We nevertheless wish that masters be held responsible for any acts of their slaves, performed under their orders, including any transactions and negotiations in their shops, and for the particular type of commerce for which their masters employed them. And in the case where their masters have not given them any order, and have not employed them, they will be held responsible only to the extent that they themselves have profited by the slaves' actions. And if nothing has turned to the profit of their masters, the *peculium* [property under

direct control of the slave] of the said slaves that their masters have permitted them to have, will be held, after which their masters will first deduct that which is due to them. If not, the *peculium*, consisting in whole or in part of merchandise, with which the slaves have been permitted to do business separately, will be split equally between the master and the other creditors.

30. Slaves are not allowed to hold offices or commissions with any public function, nor are to be named as agents by anyone other than their masters to act or administer any trade or estimate losses or as witnesses, in either civil or criminal matters; and in cases where they are heard as witnesses, their dispositions will only serve as memoranda to aid the judges in the investigation, without being the source of any presumption, conjecture or proof.

31. Nor can slaves be party, either in judgment or in civil suits, as plaintiff or defendant, neither in civil or criminal suits, except to act for or defend their masters in civil proceedings and to pursue in criminal matters the reparation of insults or excesses that are committed against their slaves.

32. Slaves may be prosecuted criminally, without implicating their master, unless he is an accomplice. Accused slaves will be judged in the first instance by ordinary judges and under appeal to the sovereign council, upon the same instruction, and with the same formalities as free people.

[Articles 33–37 stated that the death sentence is the ultimate punishment for slaves who commit crimes, from bruising or causing a member of the master's family to bleed to assault against any free person or theft of valuable property. For misdemeanors, such as theft of food, slaves could be beaten or branded. Masters could also be fined for their slaves' crimes against others.]

38. A fugitive slave who has been in hiding for a month, counting from the day that his master made a public announcement, will have his ears cut off and be branded with the fleur-de-lis [a symbol of the king of France] on his shoulder. For recidivism for another month, likewise counting from the date of a public announcement, he will be hamstrung and branded on the other shoulder with the fleur-de-lis. For the third time, he will be condemned to death.

39. Former slaves, now free, who have harbored runaway slaves in their houses are condemned as a group to pay a fine of 3,000

pounds of sugar to the masters for each day of harboring slaves. Other free people who have similarly harbored runaway slaves must pay a fine of ten *livres turnois* [French unit of money] for each day of retention.

[Articles 40–41 established procedures whereby slaves sentenced to death would have their cases reviewed by governmental appointees and prohibited judges from receiving fees for deciding these cases. Articles 42–43 set limits on the violence masters could use against their slaves. Shackling, beating, and whipping slaves were permitted; mutilation and killing were not. Articles 44–54 regulated slaves as a particular type of property, including provisions for their status as inheritance (they were heritable) and a prohibition against their seizure against a debt. Husbands, wives, and children could not be sold separately.]

55. Masters, having reached the age of twenty, will be able to manumit their slaves by all deeds or by cause of death, without being required to provide the reason for this manumission; neither will they need the parents' permission, provided that they are over twenty-five years of age.

56. Slaves who have been made universal beneficiaries by their masters, or named executors of their masters' testaments or tutors of their children will be held and regarded as manumitted.

57. We declare slaves' manumissions enacted in our islands to serve in place of birth in our islands and manumitted slaves will not need our letters of naturalization in order to enjoy the advantages of our natural subjects in our kingdom, lands, and countries under our obedience, even if they were born in foreign lands.

58. We command manumitted slaves to retain a particular respect for their former masters, their widows, and their children; such that any insult will be punished more severely than if it had been done to another person. We nevertheless declare them free and absolved of any other burdens, services or rights that their former masters would like to claim, as much on their persons as on their possessions and estates as patrons.

59. We grant to manumitted slaves the same rights, privileges and liberties enjoyed by persons born free. We wish that they merit this acquired liberty and that it produce in them, both for their persons and for their property, the same effects that the good fortune of natural liberty causes in our other subjects.

This we give and command to our loved and loyal supporters the persons holding our sovereign council established in Martinique, Guadeloupe, and Saint-Christophe, that they have it read, published, and registered. . . .

[Signed Louis, Colbert, LeTellier]

2

A Tavern Keeper Sues for Her Freedom in Martinique (Binture v. La Pallu)

1705–1714

A slave woman, Babet Binture, claimed freedom from her mistress, Madame La Pallu, on the grounds that she had been free since birth. Although some facts are murky, the surviving documents show a real power struggle — not only between slave and mistress, but also between royal officials on the island of Martinique and the crown itself in France. Historians have not found any surviving documents, such as baptismal records, to confirm or deny Binture's claim. The case stretched out over the better part of a decade, and we do not know the final outcome. However, it is significant that Binture was able to persuade at least one official of the legitimacy of her claim to free status.

The first letter excerpted below, from the Governor of Martinique to the French secretary of state, provides useful background to Binture's case.

Governor Machault, Letter to the Secretary of State for the Marine, August 30, 1704

Whereas the free Negroes harbor runaway slaves to work in their gardens, they conceal the goods they've stolen, and they even share these thefts with them, and in this they do wrongs that are very harmful to the colonists. To bring a remedy to this I believe, Your Grace, that it would be in the interest of justice to publish an ordinance to the effect that free Negroes who are found to be harboring runaways will

French National Archives, Col. C^8 A 15, f. 268v–69v. Translated by Sue Peabody.

be deprived of their freedom and that they and their entire family residing with them will be sold to the King's profit. This will make it impossible for slaves to run away.

With regard to the free Negroes, there is another abuse that must be remedied. There are masters who free their Negresses after having "abused" them and lower-class whites [*petits habitants*] who allow their slaves to purchase their freedom for silver, which encourages the slaves to steal to make the price of their freedom, I believe. My Grace, to stop these abuses one could order that no master could free his slaves without the permission of the Sovereign Council, which would judge whether there is a valid reason to allow them to enjoy this grace. This precaution would prevent freedom from becoming the reward for theft and impurity.

Your very humble and very obedient servant,
De Machault
Fort Royal, Martinique

Acting Intendant Mithon, Judgment on Babet Binture's Petition for Freedom, April 8, 1705

Seen by me, the Intendant, the petition presented to Machault, Governor, by Babet Binture, Negress, which was forwarded to us by the said Babet, who is presently in the service of Miss La Pallu. By this petition, she seeks her liberty, claiming to have been born of a free father and a free mother. . . . Heard: the said Miss Pallu and the said Binture, who requested us to hear witnesses that they have produced on both sides. . . . Received and viewed: the depositions of the said witnesses and notably the grandchildren of Mrs. Chauvigny, resident of Saint Barthelemy, owner of Big John, father of the said Babet Binture and of her family. All of which having been diligently examined and the said Babet Binture not having been able to produce any ticket nor justifying evidence for the claimed freedom, which she has never enjoyed until now, we have ~~condemned~~ [scratched out in the original document] dismissed and do dismiss the pretensions to the said liberty, declare her a slave of the said Miss Pallu and, to punish her temerity to start inappropriate and groundless proceedings against the said Miss Pallu, her mistress, we have condemned and do condemn

French National Archives, Col. F^3 250, p. 301. Translated by Sue Peabody.

[her] to submit to a month in prison, feet in chains, in the royal prisons of this island. . . .

Given in the village of St. Pierre of Martinique
Signed, Mithon
[Acting Intendant]

Intendant Vaucresson, Pronouncement, August 25, 1708

Binture's sister, Catin Lamy, was recognized as free since birth by the Martinique Superior Council in May 1708. At the time, Lamy was residing with "the widow Begue near the Grand Church."

Later that summer, the public prosecutor, Jean Doussin, petitioned the new intendant, Vaucresson, stating that since the Superior Council had recognized Catin as free since birth, her sister must also necessarily be free.

Madame La Pallu filed two separate petitions asserting her continued ownership of Binture. Vaucresson ordered the Superior Council to hold new hearings, and Vaucresson gave the following decision, delivered to Madame La Pallu's son.

We, without regard for the judgment of Sir Mithon, considering the inquiries which were made since then, declared and declare the said Babet, Negress, and all her children free and emancipated from birth, to enjoy their freedom like the other freedmen. We further order that the said Dame La Pallu give the said Babet and the children back to the public prosecutor.

Summon[ed] and given in Martinique, 25 August 1708.
Signed Arnoult de Vaucresson

French National Archives, Col. F³ 250, pp. 305–7. Translated by Sue Peabody.

Governor Phélypeaux, Letter to the Secretary of State for the Marine, April 6, 1713

Following the intendant's decision, Babet Binture moved to the home of "Dame widow Begue." Two years later, the secretary of state in Versailles wrote to Vaucresson in severe tones, warning that his overturning of Acting Intendant Mithon's 1705 decision (finding Babet to be a slave) had not followed proper procedures. Still, he relented, "as the Superior Council has found evidence in support of Babet's liberty, His Majesty finds the substance of the finding correct, if very irregular in form." Thus Babet Binture's freedom had been ratified all the way up through the French royal administrative apparatus. The case appeared to be closed.

And yet, Babet Binture's ordeal was not over. In 1709, a new governor, Phélypeaux, replaced Machault, who had died in office. Governor Phélypeaux was the cousin of his superior, Secretary of State for the Marine Pontchartrain. In the spring of 1713, Phélypeaux wrote to Pontchartrain.

A short time after my arrival here I received repeated complaints regarding a glaringly unjust case, which has reduced a woman and her children to begging. She is the widow of a gentleman named La Pallu. The first memorandum that was presented to me came fairly early by way of the Intendant because that is almost all he has spoken of to me, for he is the principle or perhaps the only party in this affair. The Intendant told me that you have been notified of his judgment in this matter and that you have approved of it. After which he brought me proof in the form of an extract of one of your letters, so I kept my mouth shut. I did not want to meddle further in this affair and I said so to Madame La Pallu in returning her petition to her.

Soon thereafter I learned of such disorders in all matters here in Guadeloupe and Grenada that I tried my best to redress them. . . . That of Madame La Pallu stands out above all others. . . . Even supposing that the extract of one of your letters to the Intendant is genuine, I understood that what you had decided was based upon what he had decided to show you because—most certainly—if he had told you the whole truth, you would have reached a different decision. . . . What follows is the complete, unadorned truth, without prejudice or intervention on my part. . . .

French National Archives, Col. C⁸ A 19, f. 80–85v. Translated by Sue Peabody.

The Negress Babet, surnamed "La Pallu" after the name of the woman whose slave she is, found access to the Intendant by means of another Negress, her sister, named Marie, who has returned to Martinique from her stay with the English, who gave her her freedom in Jamaica. . . . This Negress Marie settled in our village, Saint Pierre, managing a cabaret for a long time and earning by this commerce, as well as others, much wealth with the buccaneers who have shopped with her since the war. The subtle and cunning Negress Marie gained admission to the home of Madame de Begue by showering her with presents, which she still does on a daily basis to have her friendship, her protection, and consequently, that of Monsieur de Begue and the Intendant, with whom Madame de Begue can do anything. The Negress Marie succeeded very well, to the point where she and her two sisters, named Catin and Babet pay frequent and long visits to the Intendant, who gives them peaceful and private audiences, such that it often occurs that judges, individual parties, or others having business with the Intendant must wait three or four hours outside the locked door to his office. After which, not without scandal and murmur, these Negresses are seen to leave. Madame de Begue, who does not complain at all of her troubles, descends to visiting these Negresses at their homes frequently and has received light meals there.

. . . When Madame La Pallu's son, an officer in the militia, was insulted by this Negress Babet, his true but unjustly manumitted slave, he could not help himself from giving her two little swats with a stick that he was carrying in his hand. The Negress Babet and Madame de Begue, furious, went to the Intendant who, by his manservant, soon conducted the son to prison. This gentleman [the Intendant] has given no regard for the laws of the country between whites and blacks or even the degree to which such conduct by an Intendant could incite the Negroes' insolence.

On the contract of sale of the Negress Marie Castelet, newly recovered from Saint-Domingue, is the receipt for the price for which she was sold, evidence plainly demonstrating that these women were born slaves and not free as they have falsely claimed. . . .

These good reasons have not opened Mr. de Vaucresson's eyes in the least; he flew into a rage against Dame La Pallu when she presented herself with this new evidence to the Council where he then presided.

Besides the ruin of the La Pallu family, one of the better and the most numerous of this land, this judgment has caused extreme disorders in the policing and the rule of this village of Saint Pierre where these three Negresses currently play as nightclub proprietors [*cabaretières*], madams, whores, fences of stolen property and runaway slaves. In sum, every day they do everything that is prohibited by the articles of the *Code Noir*. It is notoriously and scandalously known that the houses of these three Negresses serve the village of Saint Pierre as rendezvous for every kind of disorder, no one daring to bring complaints against them or to de Begue or de Vaucresson for fear of being chastised instead of having justice because of the perfect devotion that is manifest that these two sirs have for the three Negresses. . . . I only recently learned all these details. I know how to remedy it, having charged the faithful people of Saint Pierre to keep me informed of the first disorders of these three Negresses so that I will immediately have them conducted to the dungeon of Fort Royal to distance them from the iniquitous protections of [Intendant Vaucresson in] Saint Pierre.

The Superior Council has issued an act to empty and tear down all the cabarets held by both Negroes and whites along the sea and the outlying places surrounding Saint Pierre, because of the disorders committed there. . . . I am so irritated to have to write to you of such filth, as I do not doubt that you will also be in learning of them.

To render the justice that you owe to the Dame La Pallu, and rectify Mr. de Vaucresson's iniquitous judgment, I believe that you cannot avoid having the king grant an act of revision before the Superior Council, or in front of whomever you please, or decisively by yourself.

I beg you to make me the honor of believing that I am, with attachment, gratitude and respect, your very humble and very obedient servant,

Phélypeaux
Fort Royal, Martinique
6 April 1713

Intendant Vaucresson, Letter to the Secretary of State for the Marine, September 10, 1714

I saw the new petition by the widow La Pallu on the subject of the freedom of the Negress Babet Binture and her children. I will not omit to follow your orders, that is, to receive her to a new test of proofs, and I will inform you of what I do on this subject. You must, however, be persuaded that this will take place without presumption on my part, as I have for this widow all the regard that justice will demand.

French National Archives, Col. C⁸ A 20, f. 87v–89. Translated by Sue Peabody.

3

French Royal Decree on Manumitting Slaves

October 24, 1713

The Binture case stimulated the French royal government to issue increasingly strict regulations on manumission. In 1711, Governor Phélypeaux of Martinique urged the secretary of state in Versailles to restrict colonists' rights to manumit their slaves as laid out in the 1685 Code Noir. Intendant Vaucresson objected, but the king responded with the following decree.

His majesty has, by his Law of March 1685 concerning the Slaves of the Islands of America [the *Code Noir*], Article 55, ordained that masters could manumit their slaves by all legal deeds, or by cause of death, without their being held to provide a reason for the manumission, nor that they need to seek the advice of relatives, even when they are minors under the age of twenty-five; but the custom has been known that since then a much greater number of slaves has arrived in

M. L. E. Moreau de Saint-Méry, *Loix et constitutions des colonies françoises de l'Amérique sous le vent*, 6 vols. (Paris, 1784–[1790]), 2:398–99. Translated by Sue Peabody.

the islands and the number of settlements has grown considerably; many abuses have been and are now committed through the greed of many colonists who, without any other motive than their avarice, free their Negro slaves for a cash price. This then leads slaves to undertake the most illicit acts to procure for themselves the necessary sums to obtain this liberty. And, desiring to act upon it and to prevent the mercenary masters from indiscriminately giving their slaves their freedom for cash, which entices them into theft and disorder: His Majesty has ordained and does ordain that in the future it will not be permitted for any person, no matter what their quality or status, to free their slaves without first having obtained the written permission of: for the Windward Islands, the Governor-General and the Intendant of the Islands; for the islands of La Tortue and the coast of Saint-Domingue, Guyana and the island of Cayenne, the local Governor and Superintendent-Director. These will issue their permissions at no cost when the motives expressed by the masters who want to manumit their slaves appear legitimate. His Majesty wishes that any manumissions made in the future without these permissions will be null and that the freedmen may not enjoy them nor be recognized as such. On the contrary, His Majesty orders that they be held, supposed and reputed to be slaves, that they be confiscated from their masters and sold for the profit of His Majesty. Nevertheless, His Majesty does not wish this to apply to slaves who were manumitted prior to the present law, by consequence of the Law of March 1685; these he wishes to enjoy their freedom, in conformance with the said law, and that they be recognized and held as free. In addition, His Majesty ordains that the said Law of March 1685 be executed according to its form and substance, in those aspects not departing from subsequent laws. His Majesty enjoins the Governors and Lieutenants-General, the local Governors, the Intendant, and the Superintendent-Directors of the said Islands and all other officers to enforce it, at the execution of the present Law, which will be registered, published, and posted, etc.

Registered by the Council of Cap-Français, Saint-Domingue, 2 January 1714 and that of Petit Goave, Saint-Domingue, 5 September 1735.

4

Saint-Domingue Council Manumits a Slave over the Objections of His Owner

August 6, 1708

Saint-Domingue underwent a dynamic social and economic transformation in the eighteenth century as the fertile plains and lower elevations of the otherwise mountainous island were put into the cultivation of indigo, coffee, and especially sugar. For much of the century, Saint-Domingue had the feeling of a frontier land, with many immigrants hoping to get rich quickly through the purchase of land and slaves, a handful of cities full of transients with few ties to a permanent community, and little policing on the part of the Church or the French state. In this fluid environment, many French laws were ignored in practice, and a more local sense of justice prevailed than in smaller island colonies, such as Martinique.

This ruling was handed down by the council of the city of Cap-Français, the largest commercial center of Saint-Domingue.

Seen by the Council: the extract of the letter written by Monsieur the Count of Choiseul, Governor of the Island of La Tortue and the Coast of Saint-Domingue, presented by Monsieur de Barrere, King's Lieutenant and Commander of Cap-Français, stating that the Negro, named Louis La Ronnerie, slave of Madame de Graffe, be declared free; and seen: the conclusions of the king's attorney general on the same; the council, after having given the freedom of a Negro named Louis La Ronnerie much deliberation, belonging to Madame de Graffe, and seen: the service rendered by him to the king and the colony. The said Council declares him free from the present time forward in recompense for the said service, in arresting and killing the one named Baguedy, Negro slave belonging to Sir Skeret, and the one named la Boullaye, Negro belonging to Dame Dureau, and having put under arrest, by the means of his comrades, other Negroes and Negresses in the company and plot of the said Baguedy, sought and

M. L. E. Moreau de Saint-Méry, *Loix et constitutions des colonies françoises de l'Amérique sous le vent*, 6 vols. (Paris, 1784–[1790]), 2:127. Translated by Sue Peabody.

convicted of murders and public thefts, the monetary assessment of the said Negro Louis de la Ronnerie made in advance by Sirs Bonnefoy, Captain of the Cavalry, and Joseph Garien as arbiters, and, as sub-arbiter, Sir Jean Fournier of Limonade, [Saint-Domingue], who took an oath before Monsieur Roger, Counselor in this Council, to well and faithfully give the said evaluation, which will be levied on the Public and placed in the hands of the one to whom it belongs, and that the said Negro Louis will remain in the service of the said Dame until she has received the price of the said assessment.

The Dame de Graffe made a petition to the Council, holding that the death of Baguedy should not be attributed to her Negro, and that, moreover, her slave cannot be freed without her consent, which she refuses to give. By the Act of 2 July 1709, her petition was rejected, which added to the triumph of La Ronnerie, who then had the grateful public as his defender.

5

France's Freedom Principle and Race

1759

In 1759, the Parlement of Paris ruled, for its first and last time, on the status of slaves in France. The case is peculiar in that the slave in question, Francisque, came not from the heart of France's slave empire in the Americas, but rather from its outpost in India, Pondichéry.

The Parlement heard this case on appeal. The lower Admiralty Court had ruled in favor of the slave, ordering his master, Sir Brignon, to pay Francisque 800 livres for eight years' back wages, plus 200 livres in interest and damages for his imprisonment during the trial.

This document is Francisque's lawyers' argument from that appeal. It was not unusual for lawyers to distribute pamphlets summarizing their cases throughout Paris. These pamphlets were designed to stir up public opinion, and—unlike all other publications in France—they were not subject to royal censorship.

Mémoire signifié pour le nommé Francisque, Indien de nation, néophyte de l'Eglise Romain, contre le Sieur Allain-François-Ignace Brignon, se disant Ecuyer, Appellant. Translated by Sue Peabody.

Lawyers' Argument for Francisque, of the Nation of India, Novice in the Roman Catholic Church, Defendant, against Sir Allain François Ignace Brignon, Calling Himself "Esquire," Appellant, Paris, France, 1759

FACTS

Can an Indian, a native of Pondichéry under French rule, who has been subjected to the rigors of slavery from the age of eight years and since then enlightened to the Christian truths and devoted to their practice, can he, after ten years of residence in France, justifiably claim to have acquired the freedom that this monarchy offers? Can he legitimately believe himself to be freed from the yoke of servitude against a nomadic Frenchman who, without any intention of returning to the Indies, has for the same eight years lived in Paris? This is the interesting question that has pitted misery against opulence: a question that has already been decided in favor of the slaves of America, for whom our sovereigns have pronounced laws. But it is a relatively new question with regard to Indians because, born free, nowhere in the archives of justice can be found any individual guidance regarding their emancipation in this kingdom.

France, this land where the privileges of humanity have for their fundamental principle the laws of nature, where the purest sentiment is the soul of the legislation, France is homeland of Sir Brignon. He was born in the city of Saint Malo in northwestern France. Little favored by fortune, he felt a commendable desire: to cross the seas. He was drawn to distant countries to find treasures that he had not discovered at his own hearth. By his own industry he made up for what he lacked in inheritance. If only his useful talents—which can only be honored—had remained untouched by the pride and arrogance of upstarts! Then he would not have to fight the natural and wise laws of his country today.

Around the year 1747 or 1748, Sir Brignon was in Pondichéry in the East Indies and already preparing to return to France when he came up with an extravagant plan to introduce slavery to this free nation. Drunk with the pleasure of astonishing his compatriots' eyes with the riches he had acquired in his travels, he bought two young black Indians for the sum of five rupees each. Their first assignment was as decoration of a procession during his voyage to the too-celebrated capital of Portugal. Then, as he could extract no more useful service from them because they were so young, he sent them to his mother in Saint Malo. She carefully had them instructed in the Catholic faith and they were baptized.

After two or three years, Sir Brignon returned to his homeland loaded with rather considerable goods to establish himself and live honorably. His ambition apparently satisfied (or at least not permitting him to undertake any further long-distance journeys), he came to establish himself in the capital, in the center of luxurious opulence. . . . He bought an elevated and dominating plot [in Paris]. There he built a kind of castle, laid out formal gardens, planted groves. In a word, nothing was spared to make a sumptuous residence.

From 1750, when Sir Brignon established himself in this city, until 1757, he had in his service the two Indians. . . . He claims that he always planned to send them back to the French colonies and, since their arrival in Saint Malo, he annually registered them with the Admiralty Clerk as the *Code Noir* requires of American merchants who bring slaves to France with the intention of returning them to the colonies. . . . As will be shown, these registrations are insufficient, irregular, and of no effect by themselves.

. . . At last, reason began to kindle within [the Indians]; the spark of natural liberty, the love of which is born in all men, soon made itself felt. Soon they sought to achieve the condition of their neighboring domestic servants. The condition of our valets appeared to them fortunate, compared to their own. They looked for other masters, masters that they could leave if they were not treated well.

It is well known that Indian Blacks, quite unlike the Negroes of Africa, are usually good domestics. Consequently, these two young men found new positions immediately. Two months passed since Francisque entered the service of Sir Mersent—who was completely satisfied with him—when he was suddenly abducted and sent to the Bicêtre prison by means of a King's Order which Sir Brignon obtained under false pretenses.

On 4 February 1758, Mr. Collet, the king's attorney general (who donated his efforts without cost to this unfortunate as well as to his comrade André) presented a petition on behalf of these two Indians to the Admiralty Court. . . .

While waiting for the Admiralty Court to rule on the case, André disappeared, never to be heard from again. On June 16, 1758, the Admiralty Court ruled in Francisque's favor.

Francisque's lawyers, Joly de Fleury, De la Roue, and Collet, wanted

*the Parlement of Paris to sustain the Admiralty Court's ruling on several
grounds. Beginning with natural law, they asserted that freedom is a
"gift of nature" that can only be infringed upon by the laws of men. They
then surveyed the wide prevalence of slavery in human history and
attributed its gradual cessation in Europe to the expansion of Christianity. Turning to the debates surrounding the origins of the name "France"
and reviewing the history of French kings offering protection to serfs and
slaves as early as 1141 C.E., Francisque's lawyers offered the following
argument.*

Some, seeing in the term "France" the corruption of *franche* [i.e.,
"free"] have thought that the name of the crown derives from the term
Terre franche ["free land"]. Others believe that it comes from the Teu-
tonic word *Frank*, which, in its literal translation means "free." Finally,
others trace the word to two German words, *Frein* and *Hans*, which
together mean "free heroes." All these ideas come together in the
notion that the liberty that one breathes in these climates announces
itself to all the nations because it is impossible to name this Monarchy
without having the word "freedom" on one's lips. . . .

Two reflections are enough to destroy the arguments of Sir
Brignon. (1) The laws comprising the *Code Noir* have nothing to do
with Indians, a free people. They were only published for America and
not the other countries where the trade of Negro slaves is tolerated.
(2) Even supposing Francisque were American or African, his slavery
ceased the moment that he entered France because Sir Brignon failed
to fulfill the formalities of the laws of 1716 and 1738.

FIRST ARGUMENT

The Indians are a free people. The yoke of slavery was never imposed
upon them. Sir Brignon alludes to this fact in declaring that he bought
Francisque from the child's mother. If this mother had not been free,
she could not have sold her own son.

Indians, educated in various—admittedly—idolatrous sects, regulated by laws, submitted to monarchs, rich by the fertility of their
lands, perpetuated through an ancient system of kinship, have only
needed the European nations for the purpose of cultivating their lands
and regulating their cities, as they have done in America.

If, by the color of their skin, the individuals born beside the Indus
and the rivers that feed it bear some resemblance to the Negroes of
Africa, they at least differ from them in that their noses are not so flat,
their lips are not thick and protruding and, instead of the wooly frizzy

down that covers the heads of Africans, they have long and beautiful hair, similar to that which decorates European heads.

Such is Francisque: It suffices to see him to be convinced that he was not born on the burning sands or Guinea or Senegal. . . . Disregarding his color, he looks more European than many Europeans, who need only black skin to appear African.

. . . Are there laws that authorize slavery for blacks? Yes, without a doubt there are. Can these laws be applied to Indians serving in countries other than America? Assuredly not.

[The lawyers set forth a history of the introduction of slavery to the Americas, blaming the Spanish for the "cruel extermination" of the Native Americans.]

But the East Indies must be distinguished from these newly populated lands, which are improperly referred to as the "West Indies." The climates of the East Indies have been well known for many years, always populated and inhabited. Even the city of Pondichéry, Francisque's homeland, counts more than 120,000 citizens, of whom more than 100,000 are natives. The Indians of these countries know how to value the land, conduct commerce, build and maintain factories. And it has never occurred to any people to establish colonies there. All the nations of Europe nevertheless participate in trade there.

And while it is true that the slave trade was permitted in India, and particularly in Pondichéry, where the establishment of our trading company is situated, as the laws of 1716 and 1738 were only promulgated for the good of commerce with America, it is certain that, in entering in the kingdom, Francisque has acquired freedom that the constitutions of the state assure to all slaves who have the good fortune to be brought here.

SECOND ARGUMENT

Supposing that the laws concerning the slaves of America may be speciously applied to the Indians . . . , it is indisputable that Sir Brignon lost the right that he might have had over Francisque because of his failure to fulfill the requirements of the *Code Noir*.

What do these formalities consist of? *[The lawyers quoted "literal terms as they are prescribed by the Edict of October 1716 and by the Declaration of 15 December 1738" specifying what types of permissions slaveowners need to get, and from whom, to bring slaves into France.]*

What is the purpose of these formalities? It is perfectly clear that they suspend the effect of manumission which operates in the law by the slaves' simple crossing of the border into France. But manumission is only suspended for slaves from America, whose service is attached to some residence, and whose masters intend to return to the colonies so that these masters will not be obliged to purchase other slaves. . . .

Has Sir Brignon (who does not appear to have come from America) fulfilled these requirements? Not only does he not present any permission accorded to him, whether by a governor or by a commander, to bring or send the two slaves that he bought to France, but he is completely unable to present any declaration made by him to the clerk of the [Parisian] Table of Marble [Admiralty Court] upon the arrival of these slaves, despite having held them in Paris for nearly ten years. Moreover, Francisque has in his sack a certificate from the Clerk of this district, dated January 4, 1758, demonstrating that his former master never made any declaration.

Sir Brignon alleges in vain that he had been supplied by the Admiralty of Saint Malo with a declaration that he made upon his arrival at that port and that since that time he has renewed it every two years. Since when is it permitted to go around the specific regulations in the law? . . .

Moreover, it is obvious that, if Sir Brignon has not fulfilled these formalities, it is because, having no intention of returning, possessing no permanent residence in the colonies, inclined to remain in Paris, he has regarded as useless and superfluous all the precautions that would make it possible to bring or send this slave back to his homeland, and in so doing, would at the same time give him his freedom, since India, from which he came, is a free country.

The remainder of the pamphlet addressed the objections of Sir Brignon's lawyers: The laws of some regions of France still recognize forms of servitude that are similar to slavery so it is not true that there are no slaves in France; Francisque is a minor and cannot claim his manumission; Francisque recognizes his own status as a slave, and as a slave, he cannot bring charges in a judicial court; Brignon always intended to send Francisque back to the colonies; Francisque cost Brignon a lot of money—who will reimburse the price of his merchandise? Francisque's lawyers responded that vestiges of ancient servitude (such as forms of serfdom) are not the same as slavery; Francisque does not need to be an adult to reclaim his free status; Francisque became free as soon as he arrived in France—he has been wrongfully denied the enjoyment of that free status and seeks to have it recognized; if Brignon sends Francisque back to his native India, rather than America, Francisque will be free upon arrival in his homeland; Brignon purchased Francisque for a mere five rupees—what is that in comparison with the value of freedom?

The judges of the Parlement of Paris ruled in favor of Francisque's freedom, but the implications of the case were ambiguous for the vast majority of slaves in the French colonies of America. Was Francisque freed because the court refused to acknowledge the laws of 1716 and 1738, which it had never registered? Or was he freed on the basis of race, that is, as a native of India, he was not covered by the Code Noir *and therefore less appropriately suited to slavery?*

Since French judges never publicly state the rationales for their decisions (unlike, for example, the decisions of the U.S. Supreme Court), there is no way to know what grounds they found the most compelling. However, the effect of the decision on future jurisprudence was telling. After Francisque won his freedom, the number of slaves suing for their freedom in the Paris Admiralty Court increased dramatically; all of them won their freedom.

However, in 1777, the French minister of the marine found a way to get around the Paris Parlement's objections by instituting new legislation that completely omitted the word slave. *The new Control of the Blacks law* (Police des Noirs) *prohibited the entry of all "blacks, mulattoes, and other people of color" into France, regardless of their slave or free status, thus substituting race for class.*

6

JACQUES-HENRI BERNARDIN DE SAINT-PIERRE

The Code Noir *in the French Empire*

1768

This image of a black man holding a copy of the Code Noir *illustrated the book* Voyage à l'isle de France, *written by French romantic novelist and naturalist Jacques-Henri Bernardin de Saint-Pierre after his 1768 voyage to the Indian Ocean colonies of Île de Bourbon (Réunion) and Île de France (Mauritius). Though these colonies were outside the Atlantic, they relied on slave labor to perform agricultural work and followed the* Code Noir, *like the French colonies of the Caribbean and Louisiana. Bernardin de Saint-Pierre, a friend of Enlightenment writer Jean-Jacques Rousseau, criticized masters for the abusive treatment of slaves in the French colonies and also French philosophers for ignoring their plight. Perhaps this is why the black man in the picture, a former slave to judge by the dangling manacle, holds up the* Code Noir: *to show how its protective provisions were not being followed by slaveholders in the French colonies.*

J. M. Moreau inv.   Masquelier sculp.

Homo sum; humani nihil a me alienum puto.   Ter....

Je suis Homme; et rien de ce qui intéresse l'Homme ne m'est étranger.

7

A Woman of African and European Ancestry Seeks Her Freedom in Saint-Domingue

1771–1775

In the following case, Philippe Morisseau made his will to free six slaves, including Marie-Victoire, upon his death. Marie-Victoire's relationship to her master is not clear; given that no wife is mentioned in the case, she might have been his daughter, the mother of his child, or simply a favored servant. The slaveholder's primary heir, his brother Sir Morisseau, attempted to prevent Marie-Victoire from asserting her freedom. Though Marie-Victoire received assistance from a notary—a public official who could provide sworn documentation of her free status—and two new administrators of the colony, Sir Morisseau petitioned all the way to King Louis XVI to maintain control over Marie-Victoire and her daughter.

Act of the Royal Council of State, in Favor of a Colonist, Appealing an Ordinance of the Administrators, Who Would Declare One of His Slaves as Free, December 22, 1775

. . .

Philippe Morisseau, brother of the petitioner, in his death, left only one burdensome succession; he granted the freedom of six mulattoes, male and female, and among others, the said Marie-Victoire and her daughter. At his death, all of them left the plantation without the permission of the petitioner, although it was the stated principle in these cases, that for freedom to have been validly acquired, the heir's consent must be given, that this heir himself must require the ratification of the General and the Intendant, and that everything be registered by the Clerk after the required formalities. The petitioner appeals by petition to the Superiors to make the slaves return to their duty, and they will order, if [the slaves] resist in returning to the Plantation, that the police will use force to place them in the stocks or send them to prison.

M. L. E. Moreau de Saint-Méry, *Loix et constitutions des colonies françoises de l'Amérique sous le vent,* 6 vols. (Paris, 1784–[1790]), 5:653–56. Translated by Sue Peabody.

The administrators complied with the laws of the Colony by their Ordinance of February 15, 1771, in granting him his requests, and in exhorting him to ask them himself the favor that his brother had intended to procure for his slaves and if these slaves had worked by their conduct to merit it. The petitioner certainly intended to conform to the wishes of his brother; but these slaves had begun by defying him and deserting. Marie-Victoire, above all, had delivered the most insolent words to the petitioner and his wife. He wanted nothing but to make them feel their ingratitude and to make them see that their lot depended upon him. The four mulatto men, in response to the publication of the administrators' ordinance, returned to their master; and he, satisfied with their conduct, had solicited and obtained the superiors' ratification of their liberty himself.

Only Marie-Victoire and her daughter remained in revolt. The police brought her back; she was held at the bar for several days, and then she was freed upon the plantation to give her the means to merit her manumission. She ran away a second time and continued to use the same speech toward her masters. It was only with difficulty that the petitioner was able to obtain new orders. The police brought Marie-Victoire back to the plantation, where she did not endure any further ill treatment. She remained free and was tranquil for some time; but when Governor-General Nolivos and Intendant Bongars left the colony, she believed she could profit from the absence of the administrators, who were familiar with her conduct, to escape for a third time.

A notary found the means to prejudice the new administrators in favor of the mulatress. In vain the petitioner tried by his letters to explain his right over Marie-Victoire, until she should merit her liberty, and to outline the dangers that existed to favor the public revolt of a slave against her master. The notary's intrigues rendered these considerations impotent.

On May 24, 1774, upon the petition of the mulatress, the administrators issued an ordinance [declaring Marie-Victoire and her child free since birth]. The reasons for appealing this ordinance are flagrant. That of 1771, rendered by Sirs Nolivos and Bongars, had conformed to the laws of the colony. Masters are not capable by themselves of bestowing freedom upon their slaves; good order requires that the administrators judge the reasons for this act of generosity, and guard that it is never given with indiscretion. Marie-Victoire knew, after the Ordinance of 1771, that her freedom was incomplete, that she held it only if it was granted by the heir. After this consent it would still be necessary for it to be ratified by the administrators; these administrators had by ordinance required her to conduct herself so as to merit this grace, which she had not done. The new administrators had not the right to overturn a previous ordinance, which could only be overturned by the King's Council.

The baptismal record of Marie-Victoire, of August 14, 1748, where the mother of this mulatress is characterized as "free," and signed by François and Philippe Morisseau, father and godfather, no doubt had appeared as a decisive piece of evidence to the new administrators; but they should have known that this statement would have no legal bearing in baptismal extracts, which are in no way the acts by which slaves are freed. These extracts can presume freedom, but never bestow it, especially if freedom has not been granted according to the forms prescribed by laws and by formal and solemn acts. The act of ratifying the manumission of Marie-Victoire's mother, also directed in the ordinance, is no longer in force since the possession of the girl's status is directly contrary; if Marie-Victoire had been born free, she would not have stayed a slave during the life of the one who had freed her mother; he would not have given Marie-Victoire her freedom in his testament if she had enjoyed it since her birth, following the ordinance that is under appeal.

For these reasons, having heard the report and considered everything, the King, being in his Council, has received the said Sir de Morisseau d'Ester, appealing the said ordinance from the Knight of Valliere and Sir Montarcher, General and Intendant of Saint-Domingue, of May 24, 1774, making law on the said appeal, declares the said ordinance incompletely rendered, null and void; orders that the ordinance rendered by Count Nolivos and Bongars, General and Intendant of the said Colony, on February 13, 1771, will be executed according to its form and content; and that the present Act will be registered and publicized everywhere that is needed. Done in the Council of State, etc.

8

The Haitian Revolution
1791–1806

As discussed in the introduction (pp. 8–10), the outbreak of revolution in Paris in 1789 exacerbated many tensions within Saint-Domingue's society. Whites soon closed ranks and put down the demands for racial equality by freemen of color, torturing and executing twenty men, led by Vincent Ogé, who demanded full equality with whites.

When the new, radical representatives of the revolutionary government, Commissioners Sonthonax and Polverel, arrived from France in 1793, they tried to rally rebel slaves against the monarchist planters. By now, however, many of these soldiers had given their loyalty to new black leaders. The French republican army, meanwhile, under attack by both the English and the Spanish armies, succumbed to yellow fever and other tropical diseases. Desperate to recruit rebel slaves, Sonthonax issued the following declaration in both French and Creole, the Franco-African language spoken by most residents of Saint-Domingue.

French Commissioner Sonthonax, Emancipation Decree, 1793

29 August 1793

Article 1. The Declaration of the Rights of Man and Citizen will be published, distributed and posted wherever it is needed, by the efforts of the municipal governments of the cities and villages and by the military commanders in the camps and headquarters.

Article 2. All the Negroes and Mixed-Bloods currently in slavery are declared free to enjoy all the rights attached to French citizenship. They will, however, be subject to a regime whose provisions are contained in the following articles.

Article 3. All of these former slaves will go to register themselves, their wives, and children, in the municipality of the place where they

Adolphe Cabon, *Histoire d'Haiti*, 4 vols. (Port-au-Prince: Edition de la Petite Revue, 1920–1937), 3:178–82. Translated by Sue Peabody.

live where they will receive their ticket of French citizenship, signed by the Civil Commissioner.

Article 4. The form of these tickets will be determined by us; they will be printed and distributed to the municipalities under the supervision of the Civil Director.

Article 5. Domestic servants of both sexes will only be permitted to contract service with their masters or mistresses for a period of three months in return for a mutually agreed upon salary.

Article 6. The above-mentioned domestic slaves in the service of the elderly above the age of sixty, to the disabled, to unweaned infants, and to children under the age of ten, will not be permitted to leave them at all. Their salary will remain fixed at one Portuguese pistole [equivalent of about twenty-six livres or about three dozen eggs] per month for the wetnurses and six Portuguese pistoles per month for the others, without regard to gender.

Article 7. The salaries of the domestics will be payable every three months.

Article 8. Those of the workers, regardless of the type, will be fixed at a mutually agreed upon rate with the contractors who employ them.

Article 9. The Negroes currently attached to the plantations of their former masters will be required to stay there; they will be employed in the cultivation of the land.

Article 10. Enlisted warriors, who serve in the camps or garrisons, will be able to settle on the plantations if they give themselves over to cultivation and obtain beforehand a leave from their superior or an order from us, which can only be issued by locating a man who volunteers in good faith as a replacement.

Article 11. The aforementioned cultivator slaves will be employed for one year, during which they will not be able to change plantations except by permission of the judges of the peace, which will be later and only under circumstances determined by us.

Article 12. The incomes of each plantation will be shared in three equal portions, after deductions have been made for taxes, which will be deducted from the total sum. One-third of the remaining amount will be allocated to the ownership of the land and will belong to the landowner. He will have the use of the second third for the expenses of the cultivation of the land. The remaining third will be divided between the cultivators in a manner to be determined.

Article 13. Within the expenses for the cultivation of the land are included: all of the various expenses of farming, the tools, the animals necessary for cultivation and for the transportation of the commodity, the construction and maintenance of the buildings, hospital and surgery expenses, and the costs of the managers.

Article 14. Within the third belonging to the cultivators, the overseers, who will now be called "operators of the works," will have three portions.

Article 15. The "under-operators" will receive two portions, as will those who are employed in the manufacture of sugar and indigo.

Article 16. The other cultivators above fifteen years of age will each have one portion.

Article 17. The women above fifteen years will have two-thirds of a portion.

Article 18. From the ages of ten to fifteen, the children of both sexes will each have a half-portion.

Article 19. In addition, the cultivators will have their garden plots to produce their own food. These will be divided equally amongst the families with regard to the quality of the land and the amount that it is suitable to allot.

Article 20. The mothers of families who have one or more children under the age of ten will have one whole part. Until that same age, the children will remain the responsibility of their relatives for food and clothing.

Article 21. From the age of ten until fifteen, children will only be permitted to work in the care of animals, or in the harvesting and sorting of cotton and coffee.

Article 22. The elderly and disabled will be cared for by their relatives; their clothing and medications will be the responsibility of the landowner.

Article 23. The commodities will be divided upon each delivery between the landowner and the cultivator in kind or in cash, at market price, at the choice of the landowner. In the case of payment in kind, the owner will be responsible for transporting the cultivator's portion of the commodity to the nearest market.

Article 24. A justice of the peace and two assessors will be established in each district to rule on any conflicts that arise between the proprietors and the cultivators or between the cultivators regarding the division of their portions of the income. They will watch to be sure that the cultivators are well cared for in their illnesses and that they all work equally and they will maintain order in the work gangs.

Article 25. The resident landowners or their managers will be required to maintain a register initialed by the local municipality upon which will be inscribed the quality of each delivery of commodities and the means of settling the distribution of the thirds destined for the cultivators. This distribution will be verified by the inspector of the parish and settled definitively by him.

The justice of the peace will be required to maintain a duplicate of [each landowner's register].

Article 26. The inspector general of the Northern province will be charged with inspecting all the plantations and to remain closely apprised by the justices of the peace of all possible information regarding the policing and the discipline of the work gangs and to inform us as well as the Governor General and the Civil Director. This will be submitted by the twentieth day of each month.

Article 27. Punishment by whip is absolutely abolished. For disciplinary infractions, it will be replaced by the rod for one, two, or three days, depending upon the requirements of the case. The greatest penalty will be the loss of part or all of one's salary. This will be pronounced by the justice of the peace and his assessors. The portion belonging to anyone so punished will be distributed to the remainder of the work gang.

Article 28. Cultivators may not be forced to work on Sunday. They will be left two hours every day for the cultivation of their garden plots. The justices of the peace will regulate according to circumstances the times their work must begin and end.

Article 29. [Omitted in the original.]

Article 30. The landowner or manager will be free to decide the appropriate number of operators or sub-operators of works. They will be hired and fired by him under the supervision of the justice of the peace who, assisted by his assessors, will pronounce on the validity of any termination of employment. The justices of the peace and the assessors will also be able to fire the operators and sub-operators, based upon complaints levied against them by the cultivators.

Article 31. Women at seven months' pregnancy will no longer work in the garden and will not return there until two months after their delivery. They will receive no less than the two-thirds portion allocated to them during this time.

Article 32. The cultivators may change plantations for reasons of health or of incompatibility of recognized character, or at the request of the work gang where they are employed. Everything will be submitted to the supervision of the justice of the peace, assisted by his assessors.

Article 33. Within fifteen days of the promulgation of this proclamation, all men who have no property and who are not registered or attached to cultivation, nor employed in domestic service and who are found stray, will be arrested and put into prison.

Article 34. Women who have no known means of employment, who are not attached to cultivation or employed in domestic service within the prescribed time period and who are found stray will also be arrested and put in prison.

Article 35. Men and women put in prison for the reasons stated in the two previous articles will be detained for one month for the first offense, three months for the second offense, and for the third offense, condemned to public works for one year.

Article 36. Persons attached to cultivation and domestic servants may not, under any pretext, leave, without the permission of the municipality or the district of which they are resident. Those who violate this provision will be punished in the manner prescribed in Article 27.

Article 37. The justice of the peace will be required to visit the plantations of his jurisdiction every week. The minutes of his meeting will be sent to the inspector general who will send his remarks to the Civil Commissioners, the Governor General, and the Civil Director.

Article 38. The provisions of the *Code Noir* remain temporarily repealed.

French National Convention Abolishes Slavery, Paris, 1794

After Sonthonax abolished slavery in the northern province of Saint-Domingue, he sent a delegation of three men — one white, one brown, and one black — to the French National Convention, which had superseded the National Assembly as the new revolutionary legislative body in Paris. The convention voted to extend the abolition of slavery to all of the French colonies. Using the new revolutionary calendar, the decree was issued on the sixteenth day of Pluviôse — the rainy month — in Year 2 of the new nation, or February 4, 1794. In practical terms, this emancipation proclamation affected only the Caribbean colony of Guadeloupe, because Martinique was under English occupation and slaveholders and its government ignored the French emancipation proclamation.

"Decrét de la Convention Nationale du 16ᵉ jour de Pluviôse," *L'Abolition/Les Abolitions de l'eslavage,* accessed October 19, 2006. http://perso.orange.fr/yekrik.yekrak/imgabo/16pluviose.htm. Translated by Sue Peabody.

Decree No. 2262 of the National Convention of 16 Pluviôse, Second Year of the French Republic, one and indivisible, which abolishes the slavery of Negroes in the colonies.

The National Convention declares that the slavery of Negroes in all the colonies is abolished. Consequently, it declares that all men, without the distinction with regard to color, resident in the colonies, are French citizens and will enjoy all the rights ensured by the constitution.

Constitution of the Republic of Haiti, December 27, 1806

Drafted by a committee under the mulatto president Pétion's leadership, this constitution contained two hundred separate articles, as compared with seventy-seven articles in Toussaint's constitution of 1801 and eighty-one in Dessalines's Constitution of 1805. Pétion's constitution reflected liberal republican ideology, in contrast to the more traditional monarchy of the black king Henry Christophe in the north. Pétion and Christophe remained locked in civil war until the former's death in 1818. Following Christophe's death, two years later, the country came together as the Republic of Haiti under the mulatto president Jean-Pierre Boyer.

The people of Haiti proclaim, in the presence of the Supreme Being, the present Constitution.

SECTION 1: GENERAL PROVISIONS

Article 1: There can be no slaves in the territory of the Republic; slavery is abolished there.

Article 2: The Republic of Haiti will never undertake any enterprise in view of making conquests, nor of troubling the peace and the interior regime of foreign islands.

Article 3: The rights of man in society are: *liberty, equality, safety, and property.*

"Constitution de la République d'Haïti," in Linstant de Pradine, *Recueil général des lois et actes du gouvernement d'Haïti depuis la proclamation de son indépendance jusqu'à nos jours* (Paris: A. Durand, 1886), 1:169–91. Translated by Sue Peabody.

Article 4: Liberty consists in being able to do anything that does not infringe upon the rights of others.

Article 5: Equality is such that the law is the same for all, whether it is punishing or protecting. Equality admits no distinction of birth, nor inheritance of powers.

Article 6: Safety results from assistance of all to assure the rights of each.

Article 7: Property is the right to enjoy and dispose of one's belongings, income, the fruit of one's labor and of one's industry.

Article 8: Property is inviolable and sacred. Every person, whether by himself or through his representatives, has the free provision of that which is recognized as belonging to him. Whoever undermines this right renders himself a criminal against the person whose property he has disturbed.

Article 9: The law is the general will, expressed by the majority of citizens or their representatives.

Article 10: What is not prohibited by the law cannot be prevented; no one can be constrained to do anything that it does not require.

Article 11: No law, whether civil or criminal, may have a retroactive effect.

Article 12: Sovereignty resides essentially in the universality of the citizens; no individual, no partial meeting of citizens can claim sovereignty for itself.

. . .

Article 16: All of the duties of man and citizen derive from these two principles, engraved by nature in our hearts:
"Do not do unto others what you would not have done unto you."
"Always do unto others all the good that you would like to receive."

. . .

Article 26: No one can be prevented from speaking, writing, and publishing his thoughts. Writings may not be submitted to any censorship before their publication. . . .

Article 27: No white, no matter of what nation, may set foot on this territory in the capacity of master or landowner.

Article 28: Whites who are part of the army, those who exercise civil functions, and those who are admitted into the Republic at the publication of the present Constitution are recognized as Haitians.

[Catholicism was reestablished as the state religion, but other forms of worship were permitted. The constitution established a senate, a president, and electoral procedures. Trials were to be held publicly.]

Article 171: Agriculture, the primary source of the State's prosperity, will be protected and encouraged.

Article 172: The policing of the countryside will be established by specific laws.

Article 173: Commerce, another source of prosperity, will not suffer any hindrances and will receive the greatest protection.

. . .

2

England, the British Colonies, and the United States

9

JOHN GUTHRIE, FRANCIS SADLER, AND CAPTAIN CUDJOE

Leeward Treaty, Jamaica

March 1, 1739

The following treaty was the first of two concluded in 1739, after decades of warfare between the English colonial government in Jamaica and separate maroon communities on opposite sides of the island. Maroons were escaped slaves living in areas beyond the European colonists' control.

In the name of God, Amen. Whereas Captain Cudjoe, Captain Acompong, Captain Johnny, Captain Cuffee, Captain Quaw, and several other negroes, their dependants and adherents, have been in a state of war and hostility for several years past against our sovereign lord the king, and the inhabitants of this island: and whereas peace and friendship amongst mankind and the preventing the effusion of blood is agreeable to God, consonant with reason, and desired by every good man; and whereas his Majesty George II, King of Great Britain, France and Ireland and [Lord] of Jamaica, Defender of the Faith, etc., has by Letters Patent, dated February 24, 173[9], in the twelfth year of his reign, granted full power and authority to John Guthrie and Francis Sadler, Esquires, to negotiate and finally conclude a treaty of peace

R. C. Dallas, *The History of the Maroons*, 2 vols. (London: A. Strahan, 1803), 1:58–65.

and friendship with the aforesaid Captain Cudjoe, the rest of his captains, adherents, and others his men, they mutually, sincerely, and amicably have agreed to the following articles.

1. That all hostilities shall cease on both sides forever.

2. That the said Captain Cudjoe, the rest of his captains, adherents and men, shall be forever hereafter in a perfect state of freedom and liberty, excepting those who have been taken by them or fled to them within two years last past, if such are willing to return to their said masters and owners, with full pardon and indemnity from their said masters and owners for what is past. Provided always, that if they are not willing to return, they shall remain in subjection to Captain Cudjoe and in friendship with us, according to the form and tenor of this treaty.

3. That they shall enjoy and possess for themselves and posterity forever, all the lands situated and lying between Trelawney Town and the Cockpits [an uncultivable area of sinkholes and canyons], to the amount of fifteen hundred acres. . . .

4. That they shall have liberty to plant the said lands with coffee, cocoa, ginger, tobacco and cotton and to breed cattle, hogs, goats or any other stock and dispose of the produce or increase of the said commodities to the inhabitants of this island. Provided always, that when they bring the said commodities to market, they shall apply first to the Customs, or any other Magistrate of the respective parishes where they expose their goods to sale, for license to vend the same.

5. That Captain Cudjoe and all [his] adherents and people not in subjection to him shall all live together within the bounds of Trelawney Town; and that they have Liberty to hunt where they shall think fit, except within three miles of any settlement, crawl or pen. Provided always, that in case the hunters of Captain Cudjoe and those of other settlements meet, then the hogs to be equally divided between both parties.

6. That . . . Captain Cudjoe and his successors do use their best endeavors to take, kill, suppress or destroy . . . all rebels wheresoever they be throughout the island, unless they submit to the same terms of accommodation granted to Captain Cudjoe and his successors.

7. That in case this island be invaded by any foreign enemy, the said Captain Cudjoe, and his successors . . . shall . . . immediately repair to any place the Governor . . . shall appoint, in order to repel the said invaders with . . . utmost force; and to submit to the orders of the Commander in Chief on that occasion.

8. That if any white man shall do any manner of injury to Captain Cudjoe, his successor, or any of his or their people, they shall apply to any commanding officer or magistrate in the neighborhood for justice; and in case Captain Cudjoe, or any of his people, shall do any injury to any white person, he shall submit himself or deliver up such offenders to justice.

9. That if any Negroes shall hereafter run away from their masters or owners, and fall into Captain Cudjoe's hands, they shall immediately be sent back to the Chief Magistrate of the next parish where they are taken; and those that bring them are to be satisfied for their trouble, as the legislature shall appoint.

10. That all Negroes taken since the raising of this party by Captain Cudjoe's people shall immediately be returned.

11. That Captain Cudjoe and his successors shall wait on his Excellency or the Commander in Chief... every year, if thereunto required.

12. That Captain Cudjoe, during his life, and the captains succeeding him, shall have full power to inflict any punishment they think proper for crimes committed by their men among themselves (death only excepted) in which case, if the captain thinks they deserve death, he shall be obliged to bring them before any justice of the peace, who shall order proceedings on their trial equal to those of other free Negroes.

13. That Captain Cudjoe with his people shall cut, clear, and keep open, large and convenient roads from Trelawny Town to Westmoreland and St. James's and if possible to St. Elizabeth's.

14. That two white men to be nominated by his Excellency, or the Commander in Chief, shall constantly live and reside with Captain Cudjoe and his successors, in order to maintain a friendly correspondence with the inhabitants of this island.

[Article 15 detailed the succession of leadership after Captain Cudjoe's death.]

In testimony of the above presents, we have hereunto set our hands and seals the day and date above written.

John Guthrie
Francis Sadler
The Mark X of Captain Cudjoe

10

The Somerset *Case: England's Freedom Principle*
1772

The Somerset case was especially important because it reinforced the notion—in Britain and subsequently in the United States—that slaves who set foot on free soil were entitled to their freedom. It concerned a slave from Virginia, James Somerset, whose master, Boston customs official Charles Stewart, brought him to London in 1769. After two years in England, Somerset escaped from his master. Stewart arranged to have Somerset captured and put on Captain Knowles's boat bound for Jamaica, but several English abolitionists learned of Somerset's plight and intervened on his behalf. They filed a writ of habeas corpus, a legal petition that requires the Court of King's Bench to hold a hearing to review whether a person's detention is legal. A prominent abolitionist, Granville Sharp, supported Somerset during the trial, and Somerset's five lawyers refused to accept payment for their efforts. The public—and later justices, including those in the United States—received Mansfield's opinion as having abolished slavery within the territory of England. It was a tremendous victory for the abolitionist movement.

Francis Hargrave, Arguments for Somerset's Freedom, 1772

POINTS WHICH ARISE IN THE CASE

In speaking on this case, I shall arrange my observations under two heads. First, I shall consider the right, which Mr. Stewart claims in the person of the negro. Secondly, I shall examine Mr. Stewart's authority to enforce that right, if he has any, by imprisonment of the negro and transporting him out of the kingdom. The Court's opinion in favor of the negro, on either of these points, will entitle him to a discharge from the custody of Mr. Stewart.

"The Case of James Sommersett, a Negro, on a Habeas Corpus, King's Bench: 12 George III, A.D. 1771–72," in Thomas Bayly Howell, *A Complete Collection of State Trials*, vol. 20, 1771–1777 (London: T. C. Hansard, 1814), columns 23–82.

DIFFICULTY OF DEFINING SLAVERY

Slavery has been attended in different countries with circumstances so various, as to render it difficult to give a general description of it. There are however certain properties, which have accompanied slavery in most places; and by attending to these, we may always distinguish it, from the mild species of domestic service so common and well known in our own country.

PROPERTIES USUALLY INCIDENT TO SLAVERY

Slavery always imports an obligation of perpetual service; an obligation, which only the consent of the master can dissolve. It generally gives to the master, an arbitrary power of administering every sort of correction, however inhuman, not immediately affecting the life or limb of the slave: sometimes even these are left exposed to the arbitrary will of the master. . . . It allows the master to alienate the person of the slave, in the same manner as other property. Lastly, it descends from parent to child. . . .

BAD EFFECTS OF SLAVERY

From this view of the condition of slavery, it will be easy to derive its destructive consequences. It corrupts the morals of the master, by freeing him from those restraints with respect to his slave, so necessary for control of the human passions. . . . It is dangerous to the master; because his oppression excites implacable resentment and hatred in the slave. . . . To the slave it communicates all the afflictions of life, without leaving for him scarce any of its pleasures; and it depresses the excellence of his nature, by denying the ordinary means and motives of improvement. It is dangerous to the state, by its corruption of those citizens on whom its prosperity depends; and by admitting within it a multitude of persons, who being excluded from the common benefits of the constitution, are interested in scheming its destruction. . . .

OPINION OF SOME MODERN WRITERS IN FAVOR OF THE UTILITY OF SLAVERY, BUT UNDER MANY RESTRICTIONS

However, I must confess, that notwithstanding the force of the reason against the allowance of domestic slavery, there are civilians of great credit, who insist upon its utility; founding themselves chiefly, on the supposed increase of robbers and beggars in consequence of its disuse. [These writers] do not seem to approve of [slavery], in the form and extent in which it has generally been received, but under limitations, which would certainly render it far more tolerable. . . .

ORIGIN OF SLAVERY, AND ITS GENERAL LAWFULNESS CONSIDERED

The great origin of slavery is captivity in war, though sometimes it has commenced by contract. It has been a question much agitated, whether either of these foundations of slavery is consistent with natural justice. . . . The ancient writers suppose the right of killing an enemy vanquished in a just war; and thence infer the right of enslaving him. . . . But a very great writer of our own country, Mr. Locke, has framed an argument against slavery by contract; that a right of preserving life is unalienable; that freedom from arbitrary power is essential to the exercise of that right; and therefore, that no man can by compact enslave himself. I shall say nothing of slavery by birth; except that the slavery of the child must be unlawful, if that of the parent cannot be justified; and that when slavery is extended to the issue, as it usually is, it may be unlawful as to them, even though it is not so as to their parents. In respect to slavery used for the punishment of crimes against civil society, it is founded on the same necessity, as the right of inflicting other punishments; never extends to the offender's issue; and seldom is permitted to be domestic, the objects of it being generally employed in public works, as the galley slaves are in France. Consequently this kind of slavery is not liable to the principal objections, which occur against slavery in general. Upon the whole of this controversy concerning slavery, I think myself warranted in saying, that the justice and lawfulness of every species of it, as it is generally constituted, except the limited one founded on the commission of crimes against civil society, is at least doubtful.

REVIVAL OF DOMESTIC SLAVERY IN AMERICA

At the commencement of the sixteenth century, the discovery of America and of the western and eastern coasts of Africa gave occasion to the introduction of a new species of slavery. It took its rise from the Portuguese, who . . . opened a trade between Africa and America for the sale of negro slaves. . . .

. . . Negroes are become a very considerable article in the commerce between Africa and America; and domestic slavery has taken so deep a root in most of our own American colonies, as well as in those of other nations, that there is little probability of ever seeing it generally suppressed.

THE ATTEMPT TO INTRODUCE THE SLAVERY OF NEGROES INTO ENGLAND EXAMINED

I shall now endeavor to show, that the law of England never recognized any species of domestic slavery, except the ancient one of villenage[1] now expired, and has successfully provided against the introduction of a new slavery under the name villenage, or any other denomination whatever.

THE CONDITION OF A VILLEIN

The condition of a villein had most of the incidents which I described in giving the idea of slavery in general. . . . As some of our ancient writers express it, he knew not in the evening what he was to do in the morning, he was bound to do whatever he was commanded. He was liable to beating, imprisonment, and every other chastisement his lord might prescribe, except killing and maiming. He was incapable of acquiring property for his own benefit. He was himself the subject of property; as such saleable and transmissible. Lastly, the slavery extended to the issue, if both parents were villeins, or if the father only was a villein; our law deriving the condition of the child from that of the father, contrary to the Roman law.

DECLINE OF VILLENAGE

After the [Norman] Conquest [1066 c.e.] many things happily concurred, first to check the progress of domestic slavery in England, and finally to suppress it. The cruel custom of enslaving captives in war being abolished, from that time the accession of a new race of villeins was prevented. Another cause, which greatly contributed to the extinction of villenage, was the discouragement of it by the courts of justice. They always presume in favor of liberty. *[Hargrave next enumerated ways villeins could gain manumission.]*

WHEN THE VILLENAGE EXPIRED

I shall not attempt to follow villenage in the several stages of its decline; it being sufficient here to mention the time of its extinction, which, as all agree, happened about the latter end of Elizabeth's reign

---

[1] Here Somerset's lawyer anticipates one of the opposing arguments: that the ancient tradition of villenage, a form of serfdom, was very similar to slavery and might qualify as an indigenous British legal tradition of slavery. Under villenage, villeins (serfs) owed their labor to a feudal lord.

[ca. 1600]. For more than 150 years, the claim of villenage has not been heard in our courts of justice.

HOW IT IS THAT THE RULES OF LAW CONCERNING VILLENAGE EXCLUDE A NEW SLAVERY

The law of England only knows slavery by birth; but in our American colonies and other countries slavery may be by captivity or contract as well as by birth. Therefore the law of England is not applicable to the slavery of our American colonies, or of other countries. From thence it is evident that the introduction of such slavery is not permitted by the law of England. . . . There is now no slavery which can be lawful in England, until the legislature shall interpose its authority to make it so.

ARGUMENT AGAINST A NEW SLAVERY FROM THE RULES OF LAW AGAINST SLAVERY BY CONTRACT

The law of England will not permit any man to enslave himself by contract. The utmost, which our law allows, is a contract to serve for life . . . ; but it will not allow the servant to invest the master with an arbitrary power of collecting, imprisoning, or alienating him.

James Wallace and John Dunning, On Behalf of the Slaveholder, 1772

[Slavery] is found in three quarters of the globe, and in part of the fourth. In Asia the whole people; in Africa and America far the greater part; in Europe great numbers of the Russians and Polanders. As to captivity in war, the Christian princes have been used to give life to prisoners. . . . The right of a conqueror was absolute in Europe, and is in Africa. As to England not permitting slavery, there is no law against it; nor do I find any attempt has been made to prove the existence of one. Villenage itself has all but the name.

The Court must consider the great detriment to proprietors, there being so great a number in the ports of this kingdom, that many thousands of pounds would be lost to the owners by setting them free. . . .

The gentlemen in the other side, to whom I impute no blame, but on the other hand much commendation, have advanced many ingenious propositions; part of which are undeniably true, and part (as is usual in compositions of ingenuity) very disputable. It is my misfortune to address an audience, the greater part of which, I fear, are prejudiced the other way.

Many alarming apprehensions have been entertained of the consequences of the decision, either way. About 14,000 slaves, from the most exact intelligence I am able to procure, are at present here; and some little time past, 166,914 in Jamaica; there are, besides, a number of wild negroes in the woods. The computed value of a negro in those parts is £50 a head. In other islands I cannot state with the same accuracy but on the whole they are about as many. The means of conveyance are manifold. Every family brings over a great many.

Slavery, say the gentlemen, is an odious thing. . . . Freedom has been asserted as a natural right and therefore unalienable and unrestrainable; there is perhaps no branch of this right, but in some at all times, and in all places at different times, [it] has been restrained: nor could society otherwise be conceived to exist.

Villenage in this country is said to be worn out [yet] are the laws not existing by which it was created? . . .

It would be a great surprise, and some inconvenience, if a foreigner bringing over a servant, as soon as he got hither, must take care of his carriage, his horse, and himself in whatever method he might have the luck to invent. He must find his way to London on foot. He tells his servant, "Do this." The servant replies "Before I do it, I think fit to inform you, Sir, the first step on this happy land sets all men on a perfect level; you are just as obliged to obey my commands." Thus neither superior, or inferior, both go without their dinner.

Chief Justice William Murray, Earl of Mansfield, Decision, June 22, 1792

The judge attempted to get the two parties to settle out of court because the subject was so controversial. The abolitionists, however, were determined to get a ruling on the case that they could use as a precedent in future cases.

The only question before us is, whether [Stewart is legally justified in detaining Somerset]. If [he] is, the negro must be remanded [returned to Stewart's custody]; if not, he must be discharged. Accordingly, the [documents from Somerset's lawyers] state that the slave departed and refused to serve; whereupon he was kept, to be sold abroad. So high an act of dominion must be recognized by the country where it is used. The power of a master over his slave has been extremely different in different countries. The state of slavery is of such a nature, that it is incapable of being introduced on any reasons, moral or political; but only by positive law, which preserves its force long after the reasons, occasion, and time itself from whence it was created, is erased from memory. It is so odious that nothing can be suffered to support it but positive law. Whatever inconveniences, therefore, may follow from a decision, I cannot say this case is allowed or approved by the law of England; and therefore the black man must be discharged.

11

COMMONWEALTH OF PENNSYLVANIA

An Act for the Gradual Abolition of Slavery

1780

Although Vermont wrote an antislavery clause into its 1777 constitution, Pennsylvania was the first state with a significant (though mostly urban) slave population to try to abolish slavery through legislation. Encouraged by abolitionists like Thomas Paine, Anthony Benezet, and John Woolman, the Pennsylvania legislature passed a law in 1780 to gradually eliminate slavery altogether. By one measure—the decrease in the number of slaves—the law was successful. Yet slavery lingered for some sixtyeight years. Total abolition did not come to Pennsylvania until 1848, when the legislature liberated the few dozen people still held as slaves.

1. When we contemplate our abhorrence of that condition to which the arms and tyranny of Great Britain were exerted to reduce us, when we look back on . . . how miraculously our wants in many instances have been supplied, and our deliverances wrought, . . . we are unavoidably led to a serious and grateful sense of the manifold blessings, which we have undeservedly received from the hand of that

---

Pennsylvania Law Book, 1:339. This text was taken from William Henry Egle, *History of the Counties of Dauphin and Lebanon in the Commonwealth of Pennsylvania: Biographical and Genealogical*, p. 50; reprint, Salem, Mass.: Higginson, 1991, http://www .afrolumens.org/slavery/gradual.html.

Being from whom every good and perfect gift cometh. Impressed with these ideas, we conceive that it is our duty, and we rejoice that it is in our power to extend a portion of that freedom to others which hath been extended to us. . . . It is not for us to inquire why in the creation of mankind the inhabitants of several parts of the earth were distinguished by a difference in feature or complexion. It is sufficient to know that all are the work of an Almighty Hand. [W]e may reasonably as well as religiously infer that He who placed [men] in their various situations, hath extended equally His care and protection to all, and that it becometh not us to counteract His mercies.

We esteem it a peculiar blessing granted to us, that we are enabled this day to add one more step to universal civilization, by removing as much as possible the sorrows of those who have lived in undeserved bondage, and from which by the assumed authority of the Kings of Great Britain no effectual legal relief could be obtained. . . .

2. And, whereas, the condition of those persons who have heretofore been denominated Negro and Mulatto slaves, has been attended with circumstances which not only deprived them of the common blessings that they were by nature entitled to, but has cast them into the deepest afflictions by an unnatural separation and sale of husband and wife from each other and from their children, an injury the greatness of which can only be conceived by supposing that we were in the same unhappy case. In justice, therefore, to persons so unhappily circumstanced, and who, having no prospect before them whereon they may rest their sorrows and hopes, have no reasonable inducement to render their services to society, which they otherwise might. . . .

3. Be it enacted . . . that all persons as well Negroes and Mulattoes, as others, who shall be born within this State from and after the passing of this Act shall not be deemed and considered as servants for life, or slaves; and that all servitude for life, or slavery of children in consequence of the slavery of their mothers, in the case of all children born within this State from and after the passing of this Act, as aforesaid, shall be, and hereby is, utterly taken away, extinguished, and forever abolished.

4. And be it further enacted that every Negro and Mulatto child, born within this State after the passing of this Act . . . (who would, in case this Act had not been made, have been born a servant for years, or life, or a slave) shall be deemed to be, and shall be, by virtue of this act, the servant of such person, or his or her assigns, who would in such case have been entitled to the service of such child, until such child shall attain the age of twenty-eight years, in the manner, and on

the conditions, whereon servants bound, by indenture for four years are or may be retained and holden; and shall be liable to like corrections and punishment, and entitled to like relief, in case he or she be evilly treated by his or her master or mistress, and to like freedom dues and other privileges, as servants bound by indenture for four years are or may be entitled, unless the person, to whom the service of any such child shall belong, shall abandon his or her claim to the same; in which case the Overseers of the Poor of the city, township, or district, respectively, where such child shall be abandoned, shall, by indenture, bind out every child so abandoned, as an apprentice, for a time not exceeding the age herein before limited for the service of such children.

[Article 5 provided that all slaveholders must register themselves and their slaves (or "servants for life") with the city or county clerk's office or face forfeiture of their slaves. Article 6 made masters financially responsible for the actions of their slaves and required the master to register any manumission with the appropriate officials. Article 7 stated that blacks would be treated like other inhabitants of the state in criminal proceedings, "except that a slave shall not be admitted to bear witness against a freeman."]

8. And be it further enacted, that in all cases wherein sentence of death shall be pronounced against a slave, the jury before whom he or she shall be tried shall appraise and declare the value of such slave; and in such case sentence be executed, the court shall make an order on the State Treasurer, payable to the owner for the same, and for the costs of prosecution, but in case of remission or mitigation, for costs only.

9. And be it further enacted, that the reward for taking up runaway and absconding Negro and Mulatto slaves and servants, and the penalties for enticing away, dealing with or harboring, concealing or employing Negro and Mulatto slaves and servants, shall be the same, and shall be recovered in like manner, as in case of servants bound for four years.

10. And be it further enacted, that no man or woman of any nation, or color, except the Negroes or Mulattoes who shall be registered as aforesaid, shall, at any time, be deemed, adjudged, and holden within the territories of this commonwealth as slaves and servants for life, but as free men and free women; except the domestic slaves attending upon Delegates in Congress from other American States, foreign Min-

isters and Consuls, and persons passing through or sojourning in this State, and not becoming resident therein, and seamen employed in ships not belonging to any inhabitant of this State, nor employed in any ship owned by such inhabitants; provided such domestic slaves be not aliened or sold to any inhabitant, nor (except in the case of Members of Congress, foreign Ministers and Consuls) retained in this State longer than six months.

11. Provided always, and be it further enacted, that this act, or anything in it contained, shall not give any relief or shelter to any absconding or runaway Negro or Mulatto slave or servant, who has absented himself or shall absent himself, from his or her owner, master or mistress, residing in any other State or country, but such owner, master or mistress, shall have like right and aid to demand, claim, and take away his slave or servant, as he might have had in case this act had not been made; and that all Negro and Mulatto slaves now owned and heretofore resident in this State, who have absented themselves, or been clandestinely carried away, or who may be employed abroad as seamen, and have not returned or been brought back to their owner, masters or mistresses, before the passing of this act, may, within five years, be registered, as effectually as is ordered by this act concerning those who are now within the State. . . .

13. *[Article 12 is a preamble to this provision:]* Be it therefore enacted, that no covenant of personal servitude or apprenticeship whatsoever shall be valid or binding on a Negro or Mulatto for a longer time than seven years, unless such servant or apprentice were, at the commencement of such servitude or apprenticeship, under the age of twenty-one years, in which case such Negro or Mulatto may be holden as a servant or apprentice, respectively, according to the covenant, as the case shall be, until he or she shall attain the age of twenty-eight years, but no longer.

[The final provision, Article 14, repealed all previous Pennsylvania legislation regarding slaves.]

12

Constitution of the United States of America

1787

Though the U.S. Continental Congress had declared in 1776 that "no slave shall be imported to any of the thirteen United Colonies," such lofty ideals remained unenforced. By the time of the 1787 Constitutional Convention, only two northern states had abolished slavery, but southern politicians had begun to fear the developing momentum toward abolition. The constitutional delegates from South Carolina and Georgia threatened to remain outside the Union if the constitution formally opposed slavery in any way.

The final constitution that emerged contained several compromise provisions between abolitionist and proslavery positions; other provisions simply upheld slavery. The following sections of the U.S. Constitution touch most directly on the problem of slavery.

Article I, Section 2: . . . Representatives and direct Taxes shall be apportioned among the several States which may be included within this Union, according to their respective Numbers, which shall be determined by adding to the whole Number of free Persons, including those bound to Service for a Term of Years, and excluding Indians not taxed, three fifths of all other persons.

Article I, Section 8: The Congress shall have Power to lay and collect Taxes, Duties, Imposts and Excises, to pay the Debts and provide for the common Defence and general Welfare of the United States . . . [t]o provide for calling forth the Militia to execute the Laws of the Union, suppress Insurrections and repel Invasions.

Article I, Section 9: The Migration or Importation of such Persons as any of the States now existing shall think proper to admit, shall not be prohibited by the Congress prior to the Year one thousand eight hundred and eight, but a Tax or duty may be imposed on such Importation, not exceeding ten dollars for each Person.

Article IV, Section 2: . . . No Person held to Service or Labour in one State, under the Laws thereof, escaping into another, shall, in Consequence of any Law or Regulation therein, be discharged from such Service or Labour, but shall be delivered up on Claim of the Party to whom such Service or Labour may be due.

Article IV, Section 4: The United States shall guarantee to every State in this Union a Republican Form of Government, and shall protect each of them against Invasion; and on Application of the Legislature, or of the Executive (when the Legislature cannot be convened) against domestic Violence.

[Article V, which laid out the procedures for amending the Constitution, specifically prohibited the alteration of Article I, Section 9, prior to 1808.]

13

U.S. CONGRESS

An Act to Prohibit the Importation of Slaves

1807–1808

While climate, the harsh working conditions of sugar cultivation, and— in some cases—severe gender imbalance had resulted in the need to continually replace the slave population in many Caribbean colonies, in the southern United States the slave population was able to sustain natural growth through reproduction. This meant that U.S. slaveholders were not as dependent on continuous African imports as their sugar-baron counterparts to the south. Meanwhile, events at the close of the eighteenth century signaled a turn from slave labor in the United States. In 1787, Congress passed the Northwest Ordinance, which prohibited slavery north of the Ohio River and west of the Mississippi River. Eli Whitney's invention of the cotton gin in 1793 increased the efficiency of processing cotton, lessening the need for slave labor.

During the American Revolution, Connecticut, Rhode Island, Pennsylvania, Delaware, New Jersey, Maryland, and North Carolina passed legislation restricting or prohibiting the slave trade. Beginning in 1788, South Carolina and Georgia passed temporary measures to prohibit the importation of slaves, but these were repealed in 1803 due to the high

The Avalon Project at Yale Law School, http://www.yale.edu/lawweb/avalon/statutes/slavery/sl004.htm.

demand for slaves. When the constitutional ban on a federal prohibition of the slave trade was about to expire in 1807, the U.S. Congress passed a new law, signed by President Thomas Jefferson, that took effect on January 1, 1808.

An Act to Prohibit the Importation of Slaves into Any Port or Place within the Jurisdiction of the United States

Be it enacted by the Senate and House of Representatives of the United States of America in Congress assembled, that from and after the first day of January, 1808, it shall not be lawful to import or bring into the United States or the territories thereof from any foreign kingdom, place, or country, any negro, mulatto, or person of color, with intent to hold, sell, or dispose of such negro, mulatto, or person of color, as a slave, or to be held to service or labour.

[Further articles set high fines and prison terms for violating the law and allowed for the seizure of any ship in possession of blacks, "for the purpose of selling them as slaves . . . in any port or place within the jurisdiction of the United States."]

Section 7. . . . The proceeds of all ships and vessels, their tackle, apparel, and furniture, and the goods and effects on board of them, which shall be so seized, prosecuted and condemned, shall be divided equally between the United States and the officers and men who shall make such seizure, take, or bring the same into port for condemnation, . . . and the same shall be distributed . . . as is provided by law for the distribution of prizes taken from an enemy: Provided, that the officers and men, to be entitled to one half of the proceeds aforesaid, shall safe keep every Negro, Mulatto, or person of color, found on board of any ship or vessel so by them seized, taken, or brought into port for condemnation, and shall deliver every such Negro, mulatto, or person of color, to such person or persons as shall be appointed by the respective states, [or to the nearest] overseers of the poor . . . , and shall immediately transmit to the governor or chief magistrate of the state, an account of their proceedings, together with the number of such Negroes, mulattoes, or persons of color, and a descriptive list of the same, that he may give directions respecting such Negroes, mulattoes, or persons of color.

14

THE ANTI-SLAVERY RECORD

The Humanity of the Africo-Americans

1836

The slave revolt in Saint-Domingue posed a propaganda challenge for abolitionists around the Atlantic World. Beginning in 1791, tens of thousands of slaves rose up in bloody revolt against their masters, ultimately establishing the independent black republic of Haiti in 1804. (See Document 8.) Three decades later, as the U.S. abolition movement gained momentum, antislavery activists sought to soften the memory of the Haitian Revolution to gain sympathy for the abolitionist cause. A New York abolitionist newspaper, the Anti-Slavery Record, *countered sensationalist accounts of slaves' violence against French colonists by depicting a "loyal" slave who saved his master's family from retribution in an article entitled "The Humanity of the Africo-Americans" (1836).*

Courtesy of the University of Iowa Libraries, Iowa City, Iowa.

15

A Free Man of Color Sues for the Right to Vote in Pennsylvania

1837

Following the 1780 gradual emancipation law, Pennsylvania's free black population expanded rapidly, partly as a result of the manumissions, but also due to migration, reproduction, and the state's increasing support of fugitive slaves from the South. Between 1790 and 1840, Pennsylvania's free black population grew from about 6,500 to nearly 48,000, while the enslaved population dwindled from nearly 7,000 in 1780 to less than 600 by 1810.

The Pennsylvania constitutions of 1776 and 1790 did not bar black men from voting, but it seems that few asserted this right. Over time, the growth of Pennsylvania's free black population and the Jacksonian populism of the 1830s created a backlash against Pennsylvania's black citizens.

On October 13, 1837, William Fogg attempted to vote in the general election held in Greenfield, Luzerne County, in northeastern Pennsylvania. When Fogg arrived at the polling place, elections officials "absolutely refused to receive his vote" on the grounds that, as a free "negro or mulatto," he was ineligible. Fogg pointed out that he met all the qualifications for voting: he was a free man, had been a citizen of the commonwealth of Pennsylvania for more than two years, and was a taxpayer. When the election officers persisted, Fogg took them to court for the purpose of establishing the right of free black men to vote in the general election.

Judge Scott, Instructions to the Jury

We know of no expression in the constitution or laws of the United States, nor in the constitution or laws of the state of Pennsylvania, which can legally be construed to prohibit free negroes and mulattoes,

---

Hobbs et al. v. Fogg, Supreme Court of Pennsylvania, Western District, Sunbury 6 Watts 553; 1837 Pa. LEXIS 136. Case accessed through the LexisNexis® Academic service. Used with the permission of LexisNexis, a division of Reed Elsevier, Inc.

who are otherwise qualified, from exercising the rights of an elector. The preamble to the act, for the gradual abolition of slavery, passed on the 1st of March 1780, breathes a spirit of piety and patriotism, and fully indicates an intention in the legislature to make the man of color a freeman.

As there is no dispute between the parties, in relation to the facts in this case, and as the opinion of the court, upon the points of law, are decidedly with the plaintiff, the verdict of the jury must be in his favor, etc.

[The jury found in favor of William Fogg, but the defendants and their lawyers appealed the decision.]

Judge C. J. Gibson, Pennsylvania Supreme Court Opinion in *Hobbs et al. v. Fogg,* 1837

[A 1795 decision against negro suffrage] was founded in the true principles of the [Pennsylvania state] constitution. In the first section of the third article, it is declared, that "in elections by the citizens, every FREEMAN of the age of twenty-one years, having resided in the state two years before the election, and having within that time paid a state or county tax," shall enjoy the rights of an elector. Now the argument of those who assert the claim of the colored population is, that a negro is a man; and, when not held to involuntary service, that he is free; consequently that he is a freeman; and if a freeman in the common acceptation of the term, then a freeman in every acceptation of it. This pithy and syllogistic sentence comprises the whole argument which, however elaborated, perpetually gets back to the point from which it started. The fallacy of it, is its assumption that the term freedom signifies nothing but exemption from involuntary service; and that it has not a legal signification more specific. The freedom of a municipal corporation, or body politic, implies fellowship and participation of corporate rights; but an inhabitant of an incorporated place, who is neither servant nor slave, though bound by its laws, may be no freeman in respect of its government. . . .

Till the instant when the phrase [in the Pennsylvania Constitution] on which the question turns, was penned, the term freeman had a peculiar and specific sense, being used like the term citizen, which supplanted it, to denote one who had a voice in public affairs. The citizens were denominated freemen even in the constitution of 1776; and under the present constitution, the word, though dropped in the style, was used in legislative acts convertibly with electors, so late as the year 1798, when it grew into disuse.

. . . Now it will not be pretended that the legislature meant to have it inferred, that every one not a freeman within the purview should be deemed a slave; and how can a convergent intent be collected from the same word in the constitution, that every one not a slave is to be accounted an elector? Except for the word citizen, which stands in the context, also as a term of qualification, an affirmance of these propositions would extend the right of suffrage to aliens; and to admit of any exception to the argument, its force being derived from the supposed universality of the term, would destroy it. Once concede that there may be a freeman in one sense of it, who is not so in another, and the whole ground is surrendered. . . .

[Judge Gibson argued that the constitutional clause should be interpreted in terms of the framers' intent.]

On this principle, it is difficult to discover how the word freeman, as used in previous public acts, could have been meant to comprehend a colored race. As well might it be supposed that the declaration of universal and unalienable freedom in both our constitutions, was meant to comprehend it. Nothing was ever more comprehensively predicated, and a practical enforcement of it would have liberated every slave in the state; yet mitigated slavery long continued to exist among us in derogation of it. . . .

Our ancestors settled the province as a community of white men; and the blacks were introduced into it as a race of slaves; whence an unconquerable prejudice of caste, which has come down to our day, insomuch, that a suspicion of taint still has the unjust effect of sinking the subject of it below the common level. Consistently with this prejudice, is it to be credited that parity of rank would be allowed to such a race? Let the question be answered by the statute of 1726, which denominated it an idle and a slothful people; which directed the magistrates to bind out free negroes for laziness or vagrancy; which forbade them to harbor Indian or mulatto slaves, on pain of punishment by fine, or to deal with negro slaves, on pain of stripes; which annexed to the interdict of marriage with a white, the penalty of reduction to slavery; which punished them for tippling, with stripes, and even a white person with servitude for intermarriage with a negro. If freemen, in a political sense, were subjects of these cruel and degrading oppressions, what must have been the lot of their brethren in bondage. It is also true, that degrading conditions were sometimes assigned to white men, but never as members of a caste. . . . This act of 1726, however, remained in force till it was repealed by the emancipating act, of 1780; and it is irrational to believe that the progress of liberal sentiments was so rapid, in the next ten years, as to produce a determination in the convention of 1790, to raise this depressed race to the level of the white one. If such were its purpose, it is strange that the word chosen to effect it, should have been the very one chosen by the convention of 1776, to designate a white elector. "Every *freeman,*" it is said, chap. II, sect. 6, "of the full age of twenty-one years, having resided in this state for a space of one whole year before the day of election, and paid taxes during that time, shall enjoy the rights of an elector." Now if the word freeman were not potent enough to admit a free negro to suffrage, under the first constitution, it is difficult to discern a degree of magic in the intervening plan of emancipation, sufficient to give it adequate potency, in the apprehension of the convention under the second.

The only thing in the history of the convention, which casts a doubt upon the intent, is the fact, that the word white was prefixed to the word freeman, in the report of the committee, and subsequently struck out; probably because it was thought superfluous, or still more probably, because it was feared that respectable men of dark complexion would often be insulted at the polls, by objections to their color. . . . A legislative body speaks to the judiciary only through its final act, and expresses its will in the words of it. . . .

I have thought it fair to treat the question as it stands affected by our own municipal regulations without illustration from those of other states, where the condition of the race has been still less favored. Yet it is proper to say that the second section of the fourth article of the federal constitution, presents an obstacle to the political freedom of the negro, which seems to be insuperable. It is to be remembered that citizenship as well as freedom, is a constitutional qualification; and how it could be conferred so as to overbear the laws imposing countless disabilities on him in other states, is a problem of difficult solution. . . .

Considerations of mere humanity, however, belong to a class with which, as judges, we have nothing to do; and interpreting the constitution in the spirit of our institutions, we are bound to pronounce that men of color are destitute of title to the elective franchise. . . .

In conclusion, we are of opinion, the court erred in directing that the plaintiff could have his action against the defendant for the rejection of his vote.
Judgment reversed.

[The next year, the Pennsylvania Constitution formally disenfranchised black citizens, though they were still required to pay taxes like other free people within the state.]

16

Kidnapping

1838

This antislavery image by an unknown artist, entitled "Kidnapping," depicts the abduction and enslavement of a free black man by unscrupulous opportunists. According to the original description (George Bourne, Picture of Slavery in the United States *[Boston, 1838], p. 120), "Nothing is more common than for two of these white partners in kidnapping . . . to start upon the prowl; and if they find a freeman on the road, to demand his certificate, tear it in pieces, or secrete it, tie him to one of their horses, hurry off to some jail, while one whips the citizen along as fast as their horses can travel. There by an understanding with the jailor who shares in the spoil, all possibility of intercourse with his friends is denied the stolen citizen. At the earliest possible period, the captive is sold out to pay the felonious crimes of the law . . . and then transferred to some of their accomplices of iniquity . . . who fill every part of the southern states with rapine, crime, and blood." The image and text reflect the growing radicalism of the U.S. abolition movement in the 1830s, which began to press for immediate, rather than gradual, emancipation.*

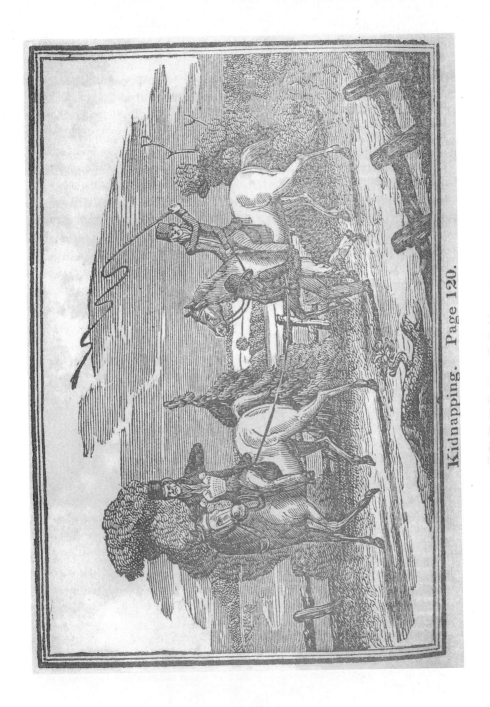

Kidnapping.   Page 120.

17

A Master Tries to Free His Slaves in Georgia

ca. 1850–1855

One of the most common forms of manumission in the United States was manumission by testament. Beginning in 1801, Georgia prohibited masters from freeing their slaves except by a specific act of legislature. Several Georgia court decisions interpreted the law to prohibit only those manumissions in which the slaves would remain in the state. In this case, the will of Thomas J. Waters, a wealthy Georgia planter with slaves living on properties in several counties, was challenged by one of his heirs, W. C. Cleland. The Georgia Supreme Court issued two separate rulings on the case, which hinged on the interpretation of the third and eighth clauses of Waters's will, excerpted here.

Thomas J. Waters, Testament, ca. 1850

Thirdly. Whereas, I own and hold in possession [forty-eight] slaves . . . to-wit: Rory, Queen, his wife, her children William and Rose, Mary's brothers, Pompey and Tom, Mary's sister Caroline, and Caroline's daughter, Dinah. . . . Also, the following slaves: Polly, her children, James, Morgan, . . . Jefferson, Cherokee, John, Elizabeth, boy Swimmer, George, girl Polly, Peggy, sister to Polly, her children, Charles, Bowling, Betsey, Betsey's children, young Peggy, Catherine, Willey, Georgia, Thomas, infant girl, Josephine, Jenny, sister to Betsey, Jenny's children, to-wit: Sarah, Harriet, Hughes, Henry Clay and infant boy, Clark, Lydia, sister to Jenny, Lydia's children, Hannah, Jessey and infant boy, Susan alias Sukey, sister to Lydia, Sucky, infant girl, Caroline, Prudence, sister to Peggy, and Polly, Prudence's daughter, Cynthia.

On account of the faithful services of my [enslaved] body servant, William (the husband of Peggy) I will and desire his emancipation or freedom, with the future issue and increase of all the females mentioned

---

W. C. Cleland et al. v. Thomas J. Waters et al., No. 53, Supreme Court of Georgia 16 Ga. 496; 1854 Ga. LEXIS 213; and *Wm. C. Cleland et al. v. Thomas J. Waters et al.*, No. 10, Supreme Court of Georgia 19 Ga. 35; 1855 Ga. LEXIS 21. Cases accessed through the LexisNexis® Academic service. Used with the permission of LexisNexis, a division of Reed Elsevier, Inc.

in this item of my will. If it is incompatible with the humanity, etc., of the authorities of the State of Georgia, I direct my qualified executors to send the said slaves out of the State of Georgia, to such place as they may select; and that their expenses to such place shall be paid by my executors, out of my estate; and that the whole of this proceeding be conducted according to the laws and decisions of the State of Georgia, I having no desire or intention to violate the spirit, or intention, or policy of such laws; and I do further direct, that if any person to whom any bequeath or disposition contained in this item offer any impediment to its being carried into execution, he or she shall, in no event, receive any part of my said estate; but my executors are enjoined to withhold from the person so opposing, any share or portion herein devised and bequeathed to him or her, and to distribute the share so forfeited among my other heirs. I desire that the said slaves, if compelled, may select their residence out of the State of Georgia, and in any part of the world. . . .

Eighth. And I direct my qualified executors, in the division of my negroes among my children, to divide the said negroes in families, so that the principles of humanity may be observed, and the separation from each other be as free from pain as possible. I also hope and pray (out of respect to my memory) that the division of my estate be without wrangling or litigation, etc.

Judge Joseph H. Lumpkin, Opinion, October 1854

. . . The first object of a Court in construing a will, should be to discover, if possible, the intention of the testator, and to give it effect, if it be legal. . . . The plaintiffs [Waters's heirs] in error insist that [Waters's intention] was to manumit his faithful body servant, William, and the future increase of the female slaves. And the argument urged with much apparent earnestness is, that the testator, having confidence that his own children would deal kindly with the rest of the slaves mentioned in the third item, was willing to leave them in slavery: but that in the course of nature, these, his immediate offspring, could not live long enough to see to the kind treatment of the issue of these slaves; and hence, his desire to emancipate the issue. . . .

Can such an intention be imputed to the testator? We cannot bring ourselves to this conclusion. Various considerations force us to repudiate this conclusion. We will advert to a few of them.

. . . The eighth item of this will manifests a great anxiety upon the mind of the testator, that the principles of humanity should be regarded in the division of his slaves—so that "families should not be divided, and the separation from each other be as free from pain as possible." Can it be consistent with this idea, that the testator should have intended to have the tender infants, the issue of these, evidently, his favorite servants, torn from their parents immediately upon their birth, and if refused an abiding place here, transported to some distant land [e.g., recolonized to Liberia]? For it is to be remarked, that the will makes no provision for the maintenance of the future increase, until they shall have arrived at the years of discretion. The owners of their parents could hardly be expected to rear them without adequate compensation, and to deliver them up, to go free, so soon as they should be capable of rendering service.

But this is not all. William, his favorite slave, the only one . . . whom, according to this view, he was unwilling to trust even in the hands and keeping of his family, must be separated from his aged wife and their numerous offspring, including the second, and perhaps third generation, and be sent off, "solitary and alone," to enjoy the fatal boon of liberty—by far too dearly purchased, as to him—leaving there his household—wife, children and grand-children, to continue in slavery! No other family of his negroes must be divided—humanity forbids this—but as a reward for William's fidelity, this aged domestic must be torn from home and kindred, and sent back to the land of his fathers!

This consideration, alone, would convince us that such was not the intention of the testator.

There is another aspect in which this intention would be equally unreasonable. Many of these slaves, it is admitted, are the lineal descendants of the testator—"bone of his bone and flesh of his flesh." Is it natural that his bounty and benevolence should have overlooked these, so near of blood to him, to expend itself upon issue hereafter to be born—begotten by strangers? . . .

We are satisfied, beyond a doubt, that it was the purpose of the testator to emancipate *all* the slaves embraced in this [third] clause. The most casual reading of the whole paper would impress that opinion upon any unbiased mind; and a more careful examination of each item serves only to strengthen this conviction. . . . The fact extraneous to the will of the blood relationship of a large number of these negroes to the testator, would remove the last particle of doubt, did any remain upon our mind.

[Lumpkin then analyzed the notion that Georgia law, unlike that of England, embraced slavery as an important and lawful institution.]

We have been strongly urged in construing this will, to lean to that interpretation most unfavorable to manumission, on the ground that the favor shown to liberty by the [English] Common Law . . . does not apply to negroes in Georgia — the granting of freedom being against the express provisions of our Statute, and opposed to the public policy of our laws. This point is entitled to grave consideration.

[Lumpkin cited prior legislation, focusing on the stringent restrictions placed on manumission within Georgia by state acts in 1801, 1818, 1824, 1829, and 1835, which Lumpkin claimed reflected "the justice, wisdom and moderation of our Legislature, respecting slaves and free persons of color. . . . Humanity to our slaves and free persons of color, and a just regard to their rights and welfare, have never, in a single instance, been overlooked or unheeded."]

While public opinion has never wavered in this State, for the past fifty years, so far as *domestic* manumission was concerned, the same steadfastness of purpose has not been manifested, as to extra-territorial and foreign colonization. The policy of transporting our free blacks to Liberia, received at its commencement in 1816, the sanction and approbation of our greatest and best men. . . . [Some] of our most distinguished citizens, continue still to give it their countenance and support.

In 1817, by an Act yet in force, the Governor was directed to deliver to the Colonization Society Africans illegally imported into this State, and "to aid in promoting the benevolent views of said society, in such manner as he may deem expedient. . . ."

[Lumpkin quoted from several decisions in which state judges approved wills that manumitted slaves and sent them to Liberia.]

Judge Joseph H. Lumpkin, Opinion, September 1855

Having concluded that Waters intended to manumit all of the slaves named in the third clause of his will, the Supreme Court of Georgia heard arguments the following year to determine whether this directive was, in fact, legal. Lumpkin wrote the majority decision.

When this case came before this Court at Gainesville, October, 1854, we held, unanimously, that it was the *intention* of the testator, to manumit *all* the slaves mentioned in the third item of his will. And the only question now is, can that intention be executed? . . .

Our construction is that Mr. Waters directed, by his will, his executors to apply to the Legislature to free his slaves and let them remain in the State; [failing this], he desired his executor to take them beyond the limits of the State—they to select their place of abode—where they could be free.

It is contended that, conceding the slaves were to be removed beyond the limits of the State, in order to *acquire*, as well as to *enjoy*, freedom, that the will is nevertheless inoperative, for various reasons: some of the most prominent of which we will proceed to notice:

First, because the election is given to the slaves to choose where they will go; and that they are incapable of making this choice. . . .

. . . True, slaves are property—chattels if you please; still, they are rational and intelligent beings. Christianity considers them as such, and our municipal law, in many of its wise and humane provisions, has elevated them far above the level of the brute. . . .

Another objection urged against this will is, that if these slaves are not freed in Georgia, they are freed no where.

Taking the whole will together, our interpretation of it is, that it directs the executors, first, to apply to the Legislature to manumit the slaves, suffering them to remain in this State; if this cannot be done, then to carry them to some country to be selected by the slaves, where they will acquire freedom, by the operation of the *lex loci*, independent of any act to be performed by the executor.

For myself, I utterly repudiate the whole current of decisions, English and Northern, from Somerset's case down to the present time, which hold that the bare removal of a slave to a free country, . . . will give freedom to the slave. . . . Still, it cannot be denied that whenever slaves are removed to a free country, with a view to change their former domicil and to remain there permanently, they cease to be slaves, naturally and necessarily. And *a fortiori*, will this consequence follow, when they are carried to a free State, for the express purpose of being liberated.

The right of removal, then, to a free State, was all that was needed to bestow freedom upon these slaves. No express power to emancipate was required. . . .

Is this will in conflict with the existing laws of this State, prohibiting manumission?

I examined this question somewhat at length, when this case was last up, and satisfied myself that extra-territorial emancipation was not forbidden by the Statutes of 1801 and 1818. I take this occasion to state emphatically, however, . . . that I am fully persuaded that the best interests of the slave, as well as a stern public policy, resulting from the whole frame-work of our social system, imperatively demand that all *post mortem* manumission of slaves should be absolutely and entirely prohibited. . . . We may not be able . . . to restrain the master in his lifetime from removing whithersoever he pleases with his property; but when the owner has kept them as long as he can enjoy them, shall he, from an ignorance of the scriptural basis upon which the institution of slavery rests, or from a total disregard to the peace and welfare of the community which survive him, invoke the aid of the Courts of this State to carry into execution his false and fatal views of humanity? . . . Deeply impressed with these views, I have earnestly solicited the immediate attention of the present Legislature (1855–6), through the Chairman of the Judiciary Committee of the Senate to the subject. Still, whatever may be the strength of my convictions, I feel bound by the construction which has been put upon the law by the eminent Judges who have preceded me, until the Legislature see fit to intervene. . . .

[After reviewing Georgia laws once again, Lumpkin returned to the colonization project.]

In view of the degradation of the free blacks, both in the slaveholding and non-slaveholding States of the Union, philanthropists of both sections favored, at first, this scheme of Colonization. . . . Nothing was more foreign from the thoughts of the men of 1818, than to prohibit a citizen from directing, by his will, that his negroes should be removed out of the State to Liberia or elsewhere, for the avowed purpose of emancipation. Neither the Act of that year nor its predecessor, were intended to infringe upon this privilege. . . .

In the next and last place, it . . . is alleged that these slaves have no civil rights—can hold no property, nor maintain a suit in Court, either at Law or in Equity, prior to their emancipation; and that, therefore, the bequest must be void for want of the means of enforcing it. . . .

But if it be assumed that a trust is void because of the legal incapacity of the slave to enforce it, then I deny the doctrine. And I maintain, that a testator may create any trust, by his will, which is not contrary to law; and that the executor will be protected in executing it. I go further, and insist, that as an honorable man, it is a high duty not to violate the confidence reposed in him. . . .

By this decision, Lumpkin authorized Waters's testamentary manumission of his slaves, provided that they left the state. Lumpkin's argument for new legislation was heeded. In 1859, the Georgia legislature banned all manumission by testament, thus drawing a harsher line between the perpetual status of slavery and the ever-receding condition of freedom.

18

Summary Trial and Execution
of a Carolina Slave

1854

This picture by an unknown artist illustrated an antislavery novel, Archy Moore, The White Slave; or, Memoirs of a Fugitive *(New York, 1854, p. 197). In the novel, a slave is mistakenly convicted of theft by a court of five Carolina freeholders (property owners). The narrator points out that since the state will reimburse the master for the value of a condemned slave, the (often drunken) court cares little whether it accurately convicts the right slave. Throughout the American South, slaves were not allowed to testify in court. However, while mob violence sometimes led to slaves being lynched before they reached a court of law, execution for conviction of simple theft (as opposed to robbery, which included violence) was rare. More typically, slaves convicted of theft were sentenced to be whipped.*

Courtesy of Washington State University Holland Library, Vancouver, Wash.

19

Amendments 13–15 to the Constitution
of the United States of America
1865–1870

Almost two years into the American Civil War, on January 1, 1863, Lincoln issued the Emancipation Proclamation, freeing only the slaves held in the Confederate States of America. In response, some 200,000 former slaves and free blacks joined the Union army.

As the war dragged on, increasing numbers of Northerners supported a constitutional amendment to abolish slavery. Some, like black abolitionist Frederick Douglass, rejected mere abolition as insufficient; they wanted a guarantee of equal civil rights. However, first the Senate and then, in the aftermath of the 1864 elections, the lame-duck House of Representatives passed the amendment. The measure then passed to individual state legislatures for ratification. On December 6, 1865, enough states (including some southern states) ratified the amendment to ensure its passage.

Public debates over the meaning of freedom for former slaves led the post–Civil War Republican Congress to pass legislation to ensure their equal rights, culminating in the Freedman's Bureau Act and the Civil Rights Act of 1866. Moreover, Congress determined to fortify the principles of equality in the Fourteenth and Fifteenth Amendments.

Under federal enforcement, the Thirteenth through the Fifteenth Amendments created new possibilities for civic and political participation by African Americans in the United States. But many whites used daily acts of humiliation and violence to resist the realization of these principles. The laws were only as good as the willingness of police, judges, and other officials to enforce them. Despite the Constitution's offer of protection, the struggle for respect and security would continue for at least another century.

Amendment 13 of the U.S. Constitution, 1865

Section 1. Neither slavery nor involuntary servitude, except as a punishment for crime whereof the party shall have been duly convicted, shall exist within the United States, or any place subject to their jurisdiction.

Section 2. Congress shall have power to enforce this article by appropriate legislation.

Amendment 14 of the U.S. Constitution, 1868

Section 1. All persons born or naturalized in the United States, and subject to the jurisdiction thereof, are citizens of the United States and of the state wherein they reside. No state shall make or enforce any law which shall abridge the privileges or immunities of citizens of the United States; nor shall any state deprive any person of life, liberty, or property, without due process of law; nor deny to any person within its jurisdiction the equal protection of the laws.

Section 2. Representatives shall be apportioned among the several states according to their respective numbers, counting the whole number of persons in each state, excluding Indians not taxed. But when the right to vote at any election for the choice of electors for President and Vice President of the United States, Representatives in Congress, the executive and judicial officers of a state, or the members of the legislature thereof, is denied to any of the male inhabitants of such state, being twenty-one years of age, and citizens of the United States, or in any way abridged, except for participation in rebellion, or other crime, the basis of representation therein shall be reduced in the proportion which the number of such male citizens shall bear to the whole number of male citizens twenty-one years of age in such state.

Section 3. No person shall be a Senator or Representative in Congress, or elector of President and Vice President, or hold any office, civil or military, under the United States, or under any state, who, having previously taken an oath, as a member of Congress, or as an officer of the United States, or as a member of any state legislature, or as an executive or judicial officer of any state, to support the Constitution of the United States, shall have engaged in insurrection or rebellion against the same, or given aid or comfort to the enemies thereof. But Congress may by a vote of two-thirds of each House, remove such disability.

Section 4. The validity of the public debt of the United States, authorized by law, including debts incurred for payment of pensions and bounties for services in suppressing insurrection or rebellion, shall not be questioned. But neither the United States nor any state shall assume or pay any debt or obligation incurred in aid of insurrection or rebellion against the United States, or any claim for the loss or emancipation of any slave; but all such debts, obligations and claims shall be held illegal and void.

Section 5. The Congress shall have power to enforce, by appropriate legislation, the provisions of this article.

Amendment 15 of the U.S. Constitution, 1870

Section 1. The right of citizens of the United States to vote shall not be denied or abridged by the United States or by any state on account of race, color, or previous condition of servitude.

Section 2. The Congress shall have power to enforce this article by appropriate legislation.

FREDERICK DIELMAN

Celebrating Abolition, Washington, D.C.

1866

On April 19, 1862, the U.S. federal government abolished slavery in the District of Columbia by compensating owners with up to $300 per slave. Following emancipation, many free blacks moved to Washington, D.C., joining some twelve thousand blacks already residing in the nation's capital. This picture, drawn by prominent illustrator, painter, and muralist Frederick Dielman early in his career, shows the fourth anniversary celebration of D.C.'s abolition, in 1866, after the end of the Civil War. On this day, about five thousand African Americans, led by two black Civil War regiments, marched up Pennsylvania Avenue, cheered on by ten thousand spectators. They stopped at Franklin Square, just five blocks from the White House, and listened to political speeches and participated in religious services. Harper's Weekly, *an early newsmagazine, captured the joy of the festivities in this illustration from the May 12, 1866, issue.*

Reprinted with permission of Harper's Magazine.

CELEBRATION OF THE ABOLITION OF SLAVERY IN THE DISTRICT OF COLUMBIA BY THE COLORED PEOPLE, IN WASHINGTON, APRIL 19, 1866.—[SKETCHED BY F. DIELMAN.]

21

STATE OF MISSISSIPPI

Enticement Law

November 25, 1865

Despite the amendments to the U.S. Constitution, many Southern states (including Alabama, Mississippi, Florida, and North Carolina) passed black codes: "enticement," vagrancy, and contract enforcement laws that limited former U.S. slaves' freedom to pursue work under different conditions. Mississippi established the following enticement law on November 25, 1865.

Although reformist legislators voided these black codes during Reconstruction (1865–1876), Southern legislatures revived the system of racialized labor control in the post-Reconstruction period. In the late nineteenth and early twentieth centuries, a system of peonage and sharecropping emerged that held many former slaves and their descendants in involuntary servitude until the civil rights era of the 1950s.

Section 9, Chapter IV. [I]f any person shall persuade or attempt to persuade, entice, or cause any freedman, free negro or mulatto, to desert from the legal employment of any person, before the expiration of his or her term of service, or shall knowingly employ any such deserting freedman, free negro or mulatto, or shall knowingly give or sell any such deserting freedman, free negro or mulatto, any food, rayment [clothing], or other thing, he or she shall be guilty of a misdemeanor, and upon conviction, shall be fined not less than two hundred dollars

Laws of the State of Mississippi (Jackson, Miss., 1865), 85.Z and the costs, and if said fine and costs shall not be immediately paid, the court shall sentence said convict to not exceeding two months imprisonment in the county jail, and he or she shall moreover be liable to the party injured in damages. *[Penalties for enticing slaves to leave Mississippi were set at $50 to $500 and up to six months imprisonment.]*

3

Spain and Its American Colonies

22

SPANISH CROWN

Las Siete Partidas

1265

Las Siete Partidas *(literally, The Seven Sections), a comprehensive legal code issued in 1265 by King Alfonso X, formed the basis for all future Spanish slave legislation. Through it, the Castilian monarchy sought to replace and transcend the local rules and municipal courts in the kingdom of Castile. With its generous provisions for manumission, Spanish slave law contributed to the formation of the large free population of African origin in Spanish America.*

Titles of the Sections of Law of Alfonso X Regarding Slaves and Servitude (*Las Siete Partidas*)

TITLE XXII. ON LIBERTY

All creatures of the world naturally love and desire liberty, especially men who have authority over others and, for the most part, those who are of noble heart.

Law 1. What is liberty, who can give it and to whom and in what manner? Liberty is the power that every man has by nature to do what he wants, except in those areas where the power or right of law

---

Manuel Lucena Samoral, *Leyes para esclavos: El ordenamiento jurídico sobre la condición, tratamiento, defensa y represión de los esclavos en la colonias de la América española* (Madrid: Fundacións Histórica Tavera, 2000), 535–37. Translated by John Michael Corley.

restrains him. And a lord can give this liberty to his slave in the church or outside of it, or before a judge, or in some other way, or in a will, or without a will, or by letter. But he must do this himself personally, and not through a representative, except if he orders it to be done by his descendants or those who are related through the same direct lineage. . . .

Law 3. Concerning the ways a slave may become free for doing good deeds; even if the lord does not desire it. At times slaves deserve to be freed for the good things that they do, even though their lords do not benefit. And this may occur for four reasons. The first is when a slave makes it known to the king or to a judge that some man raped a virgin woman. The second is when he reports a man who makes counterfeit money. The third is when he discovers someone who is placed as [military] leader on the frontier or in some other place so ordered by the King, who deserts or abandons them without the consent of the King. . . . The fourth is when he accuses someone who had killed his lord, avenges him or informs upon a treasonous plot against the King or the Queen.

Law 4. How a female slave can gain her freedom when her lord puts her into prostitution to make money from her. As to the putting of one's slaves into prostitution in [any] place wherein men give money, we establish that for such ill will as this the lord must lose his female slaves, and that they be henceforth freed. . . .

Law 8. On how one who is freed must honor the one who freed him and his woman, and his children, and in what ways the freedmen are obliged to acknowledge the good deed and to thank his former master so that he can pay him reverence. Since liberty is one of the most honored and dearest things in the world; therefore those who receive it are very obliged to obey and love and honor those who free them. And since he wants men to know about the good deed and thank those from whom he receives it, there is no way to do other than this. For servitude is the vilest thing on the earth, there is no worse sin, and therefore the former master and his children are due much honor. . . .

Article 23. On the state of men. The state of men and the condition of them are spoken of in three ways. They are free or slaves or freedmen, whom they call in Latin "*libertos*" [manumitted], which is distinguished from the other free class, that is, those born or by birth.

23

FELIPE GUAMÁN POMA DE AYALA

African Slaves and Incas in Seventeenth-Century Peru

ca. 1615

Spanish colonists relied primarily on the native Incas for agricultural and mining labor in Peru through serflike labor tributary arrangements known as encomiendas. *From the mid-sixteenth century, the Spanish crown outlawed the enslavement of all native peoples, which provided a rationale and incentive for increasing the importation of enslaved Africans to Spanish America. While the proportion of African slaves in the Spanish colonies remained relatively small, they were used primarily to fill certain skilled trades; thus black slaves often occupied an intermediary position between Spanish colonists and Indian peasants.*

In this illustration, one of hundreds by the Andean provincial elite Felipe Guamán Poma de Ayala to document the Spanish abuses of his people, a royal administrator orders an African slave to flog an Indian magistrate for collecting a tribute that falls two eggs short of the required payment.

COREGIMIENTO

COREG.°₂ AFRENTAAI,

al cal de hordenario por eosquebos que nole damitayo.

peobincias   como

105

24

Spanish Slave Codes in the Americas

1784-1789

To promote the expansion of plantation slavery in Spanish America in the second half of the eighteenth century, authorities issued new rules for dealing with slaves in the form of "black codes." Despite the title, the objective was to control the lives of slaves, not blacks in general. There were three important attempts to draft slave legislation—Santo Domingo (1768), Louisiana (1769), and Hispaniola (1784)—though none of these was ever implemented. When the attempts to codify legislation failed, the Spanish crown promulgated Instrucción sobre Educación, Trato y Ocupación de los Esclavos *in 1789, which would later serve as a model for the regulation of slaves in Puerto Rico and Cuba.*

Colonial Government of Santo Domingo, Draft Legal Code for the Moral, Political, and Economic Governance of the Negroes of the Island of Hispaniola (The Carolina Black Code), December 14, 1784

In 1783, the Spanish king Carlos IV directed the governor of Santo Domingo, a colony on the eastern side of the Caribbean island of Hispaniola, to draft economic, political, and moral regulations for slaves. The goal was to stimulate the economy, as had occurred with Saint-Domingue on the French side of the island. However, planters criticized the law, claiming that it would undermine slave morale and unfairly restrict free people of color, so Spanish authorities discarded it shortly after it was drafted in favor of the more benign code of 1789.

INTRODUCTION

The lamentable decadence that the island of Hispaniola has suffered for more than two centuries, the old abuses of its constitution and the

---

Manuel Lucena Samoral, *Leyes para esclavos: El ordenamiento jurídico sobre la condición, tratamiento, defensa y represión de los esclavos en la colonias de la América española* (Madrid: Fundacións Histórica Tavera, 2000), 1028–94. Translated by John Michael Corley.

small number of freed slaves and negroes that it possesses, whose shameful idleness, independence and pride, and the continuous robberies and disorder that they commit in the countryside and on the ranches have reduced it to poverty and the most deplorable situation, presenting a dry and limited subject for the legislator who is to propose the governmental system for its improvement. . . .

But the happy dawn of the glorious reign of our august sovereign, Carlos IV (whom may God keep safe), over the Island of Hispaniola . . . offers a new career to its industry and navigation, through the cultivation of its fertile plains, and still more considerable treasures that it produces daily in the land, populated . . . by a great multitude of settlers and negro farmers, extracted directly from the coasts of Africa, and made available to be purchased by the landowners, which will accelerate the island's return to the operations and progress of Agriculture, which should in a short time elevate Hispaniola to its zenith of prosperity and wealth. . . .

The ministers and officials must apply themselves to: the useful and regular employment of the free negroes and the slaves in its cultivation of products, so greatly needed in the metropole, and to the appropriate division of classes and races; to the perfect subordination and respect of the workers for the magistrates, their masters and, generally for every white person; the incentives and rewards for good service and conduct.

CHAPTER 18: ON SLAVE DWELLINGS

One of the major incentives for the faithfulness and good service of the slave should be the granting that, through his lord, the slave may have the power to acquire a modest amount of property on his own behalf, which will never exceed one quarter of his value . . . or by distributing to him a small portion of land for his own private cultivation, or giving him permission to raise birds and animals, or by earning a daily wage, his lords making appropriate payments.

Law 1: The good services and conduct of the slave will be the just means for the increase in the granting of land, the amount of which will grow accordingly; but it will be agreed that there be a limit, so that the slave will remain dependent upon his owner—since he will otherwise think of throwing off the yoke that oppresses him and so that he will look only to his owner for his needs.

Law 2: So that they might be worthy of the property given them by their virtue, the slaves will lose these prerogatives and rewards after they have committed any offense. . . .

Law 3: In spite of the law's harsh strictness—that the children of slaves may not inherit anything from the parents—nor from their relations nor from [slaves belonging to another master] the slave who maintains and preserves his virtue and good services until his death, may dispose of his property in favor of his children and his wife, even if they are not slaves of the same lord.

Law 4: Those who marry with a woman of another owner may leave only half of his holdings to her, and the remainder he may leave to the hospital and for the good of his soul, the penalty being so that he may prefer to marry negro women owned by his master, in the interest of the public welfare.

Law 5: The single man or widower without children may dispose of half of his property to the same establishment, and the rest for the good of his soul, it being just that, since while alive he could not enjoy the fruits of his labors, he will succeed in that way after his death, for his good services and loyalty.

CHAPTER 19: ON THE LIBERTY OF SLAVES

If a slave's freedom is the best reward he can imagine for himself, there will be few actions of value to him in themselves, and if it is just to keep the most exact rules in proportion to the penalties, there should be the same justice equally proportionate in rewards.

Law 1: The discovery by a slave of a conspiracy or plot against his owner, . . . in . . . a place where there has been an appreciable increase of slaves to a high level, or of a revolt or uprising, or a generally premeditated flight of slaves, in such an urgent occasion when he shows love and faithfulness toward whites or when there is evident danger to life, and may have saved white men in a situation such as the burning of a public building or home in the country, and his farming activities also have been of great benefit to the owner's ranch, or to a supervisor in his area; one who has fed his owner and children for a long time; the producing of six children who have survived to an age of seven years; or from thirty years of service with demonstrated love and faithfulness and exactitude . . . will be just cause to free slaves, whose valor will be rewarded by the owner in those cases which do not arouse the appropriate interest of the House of Public Taxation.

Law 2: However, the present awards of freedom for robberies made by the slaves for their owners and other excesses of like nature . . . or, on the other hand, slaves' handing themselves over for the most public and execrable prostitution in the eagerness to achieve their liberty, we forbid from now on the unlimited authority and practice of conferring freedom solely for the offering of money to the owner equal to the slave's value or price.

Law 3: For this reason and because such esteemed good would fall back or relapse if they were not people of virtue, integrity and good manners, we declare that no slave may hope for freedom who does not justify his good conduct and actions beyond the ordinary expectations and with recognition or public acknowledgment, . . . without which judges will not be able to grant freedom even if it is at the request of his owner. . . .

Law 5: And since it often happens that owners give freedom to their slaves and their children for reasons which may silence their shame, we declare that the owner or any man who verifies that his mistress is the cause of these concessions, will be deprived of one and all of his female slaves who then will be sold and the money sent to the government tax office.

Law 6: Other times, and frequently when the slave hands over a major portion of his wages, keeping for himself only a small amount as a symbol of the award, allowing him to live in leisure for a very small wage paid daily, thus freeing him from public assistance for freed negroes, and he joins either a local militia or the municipal police, for such a situation we forbid that the freedman should have any obligation to offer any amount exceeding half or two-thirds of his worth, if he has been a slave of good conduct and actions. . . .

Law 10: . . . Negroes and mulatto slaves may marry other enslaved negroes; but no one may gain his freedom by this means . . . , even if they may enter into marriage with freed negroes or mulattos. . . .

CHAPTER 20: THE EFFECTS OF FREEDOM

Law 1: Liberty gained by the slave for his good services, whether public or private, or for any money or amount commensurate with his good conduct and faithfulness, will bring to him the same effects of freedom that nature confers on the freeborn, giving him the same rights, prerogatives and preeminence as others, for his goodness as well as for others.

Law 2: For the freedman who gravely lacks gratitude and the recognized obligation toward his former owner, wife and children, he will be deprived of his freedom and restored to his former condition, his price applied toward the hospital for negroes, after being severely punished for his ingratitude and disrespect, and the slightest loss of respect and attention of freedmen will be punished in those more severely than with other negroes.

CHAPTER 21: ON FREEDOM SUITS

Slaves are accustomed to leaving the control or authority of their owners by the pretext of seeking their freedom through legal cases, by cheating [their owners] during their servitude and using it at the same time to live idly as their motive during the pursuit of their lawsuits....

CHAPTER 22: ON THE BUYING AND SELLING OF SLAVES

Law 2:.... We declare that no owner of any negro slave be obliged to sell him against his [the owner's] will, without just cause.

Law 3: But if the slave can, by extraordinary and instructive means, give evidence that his owner is maltreating him and punishing him despite his good services, or that the slave lacks the necessary wherewithal or clothing used in the negro community, or that the master imposes on him work beyond his capabilities, the owner will be obliged to dispose of the slave in the same way as if he had been seen to use violence on his slaves and obliged the slave to commit robberies or equally sinful activities.

Law 4: And since frequently it happens that in similar cases the masters are accustomed to charging an excessive amount for the price of his slaves in order to dissuade his fellow slaveowners from acquiring them and thus obliging the slave to remain under his power, we order that he show the fair value of the worth for the skills, to be verified by the ordinary judge or magistrate before whom there may be oral court proceedings....

Law 7: If a slave turns over to his master a portion of his purchase price, acquired legally, by honest means . . . with the aim of . . . acquiring his own freedom, the repayment will be noted in a certificate that may serve as a title, so that it will be clear in the event that the slave is passed to another owner who may buy him before the completion of the total recovery of the remaining amount due, unless he can be sold at a new price, based upon a new estimation of the slave's value....

Law 9: It is desirable that the Spaniard or Creole who, having had offspring by any slave and desiring to buy it, or better said, should free it.

Law 10: The slave married to a negress or *parda* [light-skinned woman] of the same *especie* [racial category] will not be sold or traded or separated from his consort, nor will the latter from his children, if they had any; for it is in the interest of the public to reunite these individuals, who will contribute to his usefulness as a farmer to the people of agriculture, unless it causes harm or damage to a third party.

Spanish Crown, Royal Instructions for the Education, Treatment, and Work of the Slaves (Instrucción sobre Educación, Trato y Ocupación de los Esclavos), Aranjuez, May 31, 1789

Seeking profits, the Spanish crown liberalized the slave trade in 1778, after which the Spanish colonies were flooded with slaves. The crown tried to impose consistent treatment for slaves throughout Spanish America through new guidelines. The goal of the Instrucción was to sustain and prolong slavery without violating the principles of religion, humanity, and the state. The decree was highly unpopular with slaveowners, who claimed that it would lead to a general slave uprising. The opposition was such that, in 1794, the crown suspended the new law.

CHAPTER 1: EDUCATION

Every slave owner, of whatever class or condition, must instruct his slaves in the principles of the Catholic Religion, . . . so that they may be baptized within a year of their residence in my dominions, taking care that the Christian Doctrine is explained to them on all the compulsory feast days, during which they are not obliged to work, nor permitted to work for themselves, nor for their owners, except in the time of the harvest, when it is customary to give permission to work on feast days. . . .

CHAPTER II: ON FOOD AND CLOTHING

The owners of slaves have a perpetual obligation to feed and clothe them, including the women and children, whether the latter are slaves or free, until they can earn enough to maintain themselves. . . .

CHAPTER III: THE JOBS OF SLAVES

The first and principal job of the Slaves should be Agriculture and other labors of the field, and not the jobs of a sedentary life. . . .

Manuel Lucena Samoral, *Leyes para esclavos: El ordenamiento jurídico sobre la condición, tratamiento, defensa y represión de los esclavos en la colonias de la América española* (Madrid: Fundacións Histórica Tavera, 2000), 1150–56. Translated by John Michael Corley.

CHAPTER V: ON DWELLINGS AND ILLNESS

All slave owners must provide separate dwellings for the two sexes, for those who are unmarried, and must see that they are comfortable and sufficient so that they are protected from bad weather with elevated beds, blankets, or necessary linens, and with separations for everyone, and at most two to a room, and the sick will be assigned to another place or separate dwelling, sheltered and comfortable, and they must be helped by the owners in every necessary way. . . .

CHAPTER VI: ON THE OLD AND SICK INHABITANTS

Slaves who, from old age or infirmity find themselves unable to work, and the same for small children and minors of either sex, will be required to be fed by the owners, unless the owners are given the liberty to discard them. . . .

CHAPTER VII: MARRIAGE OF SLAVES

Slave owners must avoid the illicit treatment of the two sexes by promoting marriages, without impeding their becoming married to slaves of other owners. . . .

CHAPTER VIII: OBLIGATIONS OF THE SLAVES
AND CORRECTIONAL PUNISHMENTS

As owners must sustain, educate and employ slaves in useful jobs commensurate with their strengths, ages and sex, without abandoning the children, the aged or the sick, and always follow their obligations, so slaves should obey and respect their owners and their foremen [mayordomos], performing their tasks and the jobs assigned to them in accordance with their strength, and venerate the owners as paterfamilias, and thus, if anyone should fail in any of these obligations he can and should be punished for the excesses that he may commit so as to bring about reform [correccionalmente]. . . .

CHAPTER XI: ON THOSE WHO INJURE SLAVES

Since only the owners and foremen may punish the slaves in a manner to bring about reform with cautious moderation, any person other than their owner or foreman may not injure them, punish, wound or kill them, without incurring penalties established by the laws for those who commit similar excesses or crimes against free persons. . . .

25

Proclamation of the People against the Purchase of Freedom for Slaves, Ecuador

1794

The origins of coartación—*the Spanish practice of permitting slaves to purchase their freedom through the payment of an established "fair" price, often in installments over a period of years—are not documented, but it became by far the most widely used means of achieving liberty in Spanish America. In 1792, some owners of gold mines in Barbacoas (in the southern region of what is now Ecuador) protested to the city council against slaves' right to* coartación. *Their petition, excerpted here, called attention to a fundamental contradiction in the practice.*

Since, . . . whatever a slave acquires is the property of his owner, the latter not giving the former more than what is necessary for his nourishment, it is clear that the slave is the property of his owner and the slave cannot deliver the price of his freedom, especially when by right, without the will of the owner, the slave cannot confer upon himself his own freedom. This is so even though there may be a third party who, for piety's sake, may wish to free him, and above all since the owner concurs in the assumption that he does not wish the slave freed, but on the contrary the assumption that the owner has been robbed of his right of ownership.

Archivo Histórico Nacional del Ecuador, Reales Cédulas, t. XIII, flos 220–22. Lucena, *Leyes para esclavos* (Madrid: Fundacións Histórica Tavera, 2000), 277, no. 807. Translated by John Michael Corley.

26

Freedom from Abuse, Ecuador

1794

Slaves understood that there were limits to the punishment that their owners could mete out. They could legally attain their freedom if they could show they had been abused by their owners. The following case, initiated in Guayaquil, Ecuador, shows the obstacles faced by a family of slaves in pursuing liberty. Cases like this, which recurred throughout the period of slavery in Spanish America, show how common it was for slaves to be treated cruelly by their masters. Appeals in this case were terminated suddenly, and unfortunately, the final outcome is unknown.

Manumission of María Chiquinquirá Díaz in Equador, 1794

On August 18, 1794, the slave María Chiquinquirá Díaz requested permission to initiate a petition for freedom against her owner, Alfonso Cepeda de Arizcum Elizondo. He was a Catholic priest whose family was part of the Guayaquil elite. Alfonso had inherited Díaz from his sister, who in turn had inherited her from their father. Díaz was married to José Espinoza, a free mulatto who also worked in Alfonso's house. They had a daughter, María del Carmen, who at the age of eleven could read, write, cook, and sew. Since Alfonso did not approve of her education, he sent her off to serve in the house of his blind sister.

After marrying, Díaz had stopped serving in Alfonso's house and had reached an agreement with him that Espinoza would work free of charge for Alfonso, and in exchange Díaz would have permission to work independently. At some point, Alfonso demanded that Díaz return to work for him and that Espinoza pay rent for the rooms his family had occupied for years. Díaz then began legal action.

Díaz presented her petition for freedom through the Slave Protector, Manuel Ruiz. The report starts by describing her mother, María Antonia,

---

María Eugenia Chaves, *Honor y libertad: Discursos y recursos en la estrategia de libertad de una mujer esclava (Guayaquil a fines del periodo colonial)*, Departamento de Historia e Instituto Iberoamericano de la Universidad de Gotemburgo, 2001, pp. 113–20. Translated by John Michael Corley.

an African-born leper abandoned by her owners, who lived by begging. After her mother's death, Díaz lived with an Indian woman until she was taken to the Cepada house, where, still a child, she served as a slave.

In her petition, Díaz argues that María Antonia should be considered emancipated, since she was abandoned. Díaz should be free "as if born from a free womb." She had accepted living as a slave only because the Cepada family had treated her kindly. When she came under the power of Alfonso, however, he had committed serious offenses against her and her daughter, including denying them clothes and food. On these grounds, they refused to continue serving as slaves and sought to claim their liberties "so coveted by all and protected by laws."

Díaz and María del Carmen were quickly given permission to litigate. Alfonso's attorney requested that the litigants be put back under Alfonso's power immediately, because "María Chiquinquirá walks as a free person without recognizing servitude, pursuing her system of using the suit that she has unjustly pursued to do as she pleases." The official responsible for the case agreed, ordering that the slaves be maintained in Alfonso's house, with the condition that they not be mistreated. Díaz, however, managed to present proof in court of her mistreatment. The notary Gaspar Zenón Medina testified publicly in support of the two slaves and swore to having heard Alfonso insult María del Carmen. This declaration served as justification for the request for liberties to move to litigation. Judge José Ignacio Larrabaytia decreed on December 19, 1794:

While naturally disapproving of the fact that the two litigants live together, though at least peacefully so, and that Doctor Alfonso Cepeda, as owner, is accustomed to dominating the two slave women, his legal adversaries, subjecting himself to the punctual observance of the two writs of September 28 and November 28 presented here, the government orders that he immediately turn over the slave, María del Carmen to the court clerk, with orders that he—denying that he was aware of any abuse of her, by certification of the clerk Medina—not disgrace her, even in public *[ni aun politicamente, se desentendió de infamarla]* and that it is therefore decided that with a small amount of modesty and obedience as ordered him, she will be removed from his house control . . . to conserve the virtue of the said María del Carmen. The case of María Chiquinquirá is to be settled equally in the same way.

[With this decree, María C. Díaz and her daughter lived "as free persons and without recognizing servitude." From that point on, the proceedings

focused on the litigants' petition for freedom. On July 8, 1797, Governor Juan de Urbina issued a decision declaring them subject to the servitude of Alfonso Cepeda, and the two women returned to his house. Díaz appealed to the Royal Audience of Quito.

In August 1797, the governor conceded the slaves' right to appeal. Adopting the tactic of delaying the process to the greatest possible extent, Díaz requested that the tribunal appoint a new guardian because the one defending her was not favorable to her cause:]

... The fact of her being an unfortunate woman and that the defendant is powerful because of his status and wealth, since the said plaintiff lives in the house of the priest, Don Alfonso Cepeda, as well as other connections which occur; for these circumstances, María Chiquinquirá pleads that your Lord grant her this petition without the intervention of the solicitor general and ... the name of the other person who sponsors her. Signed: Atanacio Larios, on behalf of María del Carmen.

[Díaz asked to be considered a destitute person, and her request was granted. As a result, the costs of sending the process to Quito were paid by Alfonso. But the plaintiff had difficulties in finding a guardian to represent her interests, and thus she appealed to the king:]

The Solicitor General of Guayaquil does not wish to defend us, nor free us from this outrage, which is nevertheless his job, only because of his favor toward the priest don Alfonso, whose good friend he is, so, my Lord, we plead to your superior piety that you will take pity on our unhappy, unfortunate souls without allowing our justice to perish. ...

Signed: José Mariano de la Peña on behalf of María Chiquinquirá and María del Carmen Espinoza.

27

National Independence and Abolition, Ecuador
1822

Beginning in the late eighteenth century, the Ecuadoran slave regime was threatened by the revolutionary example of Saint-Domingue, by slave rebellions and quilombos *(maroon communities), by the Napoleonic invasions, and especially by the new wars of independence. Moreover, the British effort to end the Atlantic slave trade and independence leaders José de San Martín and Simón Bolívar spread the antislavery message. Inspired by both humanitarian principles and military pragmatism, Latin American patriots offered slaves liberty in exchange for enlisting in the military (as in the American Revolution, the French Revolution in Saint-Domingue, and Brazil).*

Like the leaders of the independence movement, slaves incorporated abolitionism and republicanism into their rhetoric. Using the language of liberty and equality of citizens, they made new demands, this time collective, seeking not only their individual freedom, but also the general emancipation of slaves in the region.

In this document, the authors (not unlike the framers of the U.S. Constitution) seem to deliberately avoid using terms like slavery, freedom, *or* manumission, *since these might appear to give legal justification to slavery. Perhaps this is why euphemisms like* captives, miserable, *and, conversely,* fortunate *(por suerte) or* removal *(faltas), often appeared instead.*

Francisco Rosi and Others, Petition for the Establishment of a Voluntary System of Mutual Aid among the Slaves for Their Freedom, Guayaquil, August 23, 1822

My Lord Mayor,

A community of brown slaves, residents of this city, here before your Lordship, humbly and respectfully, . . . we say: that the love of

---

Francisco Rosi et al., "Expediente sobre estabecimento de un sistema mutualista o cooperativo voluntario entre los esclavos para su liberación, con la intervención de una Junta de Manumisión," edited by Berta Ares. *Revista del Archivo Histórico del Guayas*, 5 (June 1974, Guayaquil, Ecuador). Translated by John Michael Corley.

freedom being natural in every creature, in us even more strongly, as our captivity is positively painful, as are our lodgings and our jobs. . . . We beseech the Court to authorize that which we need and that, if it be denied, we proceed on our own because, in truth, we lack absolutely any advantage and the most urgent circumstances impel us to seek your help.

The proposal is in these terms: every slave who is actively employed will try to save one or two *reales* every day to contribute to a Box containing a fund for the emancipation [of all the slaves in the group] . . . , and at the end of each week, or each Sunday, he will give another so many *reales* as there are days in the week. If by the end of the first or second week there are 500 or more pesos, he will immediately give freedom with the funds to one or more of the most needy slaves, whether by merit or virtue, or by good fortune, or by whatever means it is competitively resolved, or whatever your Lordship orders us to do. In this way your Lordship will have freed two or three [slaves] with the money in less than one month. . . . The freedom certificates [*Boletos de esclavitud*] are to be collected and put in the Box . . . and not to be given to each slave until the last of the slaves are freed, so that meanwhile the same contributions as before may continue, although [the former slave] is now freed. . . .

My Lord, the freedom of the slaves has always been commendable and favored; we hope much more that the future Government will be as just, humane and equitable as the provisional one we enjoy today, that in your wise insight you will take action against our woes, and aspire to remedy them, and justly attend to our simple, quite natural, righteous and legitimate plea. . . . Our troubles and sufferings cannot be hidden from the pious heart of all Christians: but let us say in brief that the matter of being paid our daily wages from January to January, only to see ourselves always in debt—this matter is not only harsh to contemplate but even worse is to see our older children suffering under their owners, without our being able to help them— . . . these are some of the woes of great pain and affliction, so we beg your Lord's consideration for the speedy granting of our petition, since with it all can be remedied, very quickly, and legally. . . .

We beseech your Lordship to help grant our request and provide for the establishment of our proposed system, which we implore in the name of justice and without malice,

Francisco Rosi, Bernadino Arboleda, José Marí senior, José Chavarria, Simón Camba, José Ignacio Cortázar

Guayaquil, August 23, 1822

[The president asked a succession of potential guardians to represent the slaves and proposed a plan so that their demands would be met, but everyone he asked refused, alleging a range of personal reasons. He finally managed to nominate a commission, which presented provisional regulations for liberating the slaves.]

José Leocadio Llona, Provisional Regulations for the Fortunate Issue of the Freeing of the Slaves, Guayaquil, September 19, 1822

Chapter I: As to the obligations of the judge and the clerk, who will supervise the acts of good fortune [*los actos de la suerte*—i.e., the certificates of freedom]:

1. The judge will authorize the certificates, giving the order to the clerk.

2. The former will resolve all doubts before the Board, which may occur in the aforementioned acts. . . .

Chapter II: As to the responsibility of the Commission:

1. It will deal with the matter fiscally and administratively. . . .

3. It will create a Record Book to note the names of the contributing slaves, their owners, the dates and their absences [*faltas*—i.e., manumissions].

4. It will also create a Strongbox guarded by two keys, one for each one of the Commission.

5. It will serve with the judge and the clerk on the days and hours of contributions and good fortune [*suerte*].

Chapter III: As to the obligations of the slaves [*esclavos*]:

1. Each will continue to contribute a peso each week toward the common freedom fund, just as he had been doing prior to the good fortune.

2. They will not cheat on the daily wages paid by the owners under this pretext. . . .

4. They will not have the option of missing their contribution, even involuntarily, without reinstating their debts. . . .

7. All will remain obliged to contribute the weekly peso until he is freed from all obligations.

José Leocadio Llona
Policarpo Laso

José Leocadio Llona and Dr. Joaquín Salazar, Responses

My Lord Mayor,

The Commission named for the freeing of slaves now before your Lordship says that it presents the requested form as to the regulations it has created so that it may proceed with the order regarding the liberty of the unfortunate oppressed people. . . . It is impossible to present an entirely perfect set of regulations. Even so, the Commission has recommended the establishment of a very pious work in such a way so as not to burden the owners, and to facilitate the redemption of this miserable part of the human species. . . . As to articles 5 and 4 of those chapters by which the slaves are set free by means of their own appraisal of their worth, it should be made known to the Commission of your Lordship that there cannot be a more just disposition of this case than this one. The things [slaves] are to be sold according to a set price. . . . It is absolutely necessary that a slave who is now ten years old, for example, and who is valued at 400 pesos, be sold on the day of his appraisal, since his value could later decline, due to aging, infirmities or bad habits. On the other hand, it is undeniable that the value of slaves has declined a good deal, since, because of the . . . transformation of the Americas, we have begun to detest slavery, and to work elsewhere for the freedom of our brothers; and if that Spanish yoke has cost us so many sacrifices as to flood the fields with human blood, it is scandalous and horrifying that some hardhearted men without morality or humanity have insisted on selling their slaves at the same price they paid for them. . . . The integrity and wisdom of so liberal a Government as the one this happy province enjoys should resist such [an] unseemly monstrosity; as when one tries to sell his slave. . . . In such happy times, no slave believes his miserable state is just, and he yearns with all eagerness as never before for his freedom: these are the acts such as this one, to which men are obliged even if it be against their will.

Guayaquil, September 29, 1822
José Leocadio Llona

Guayaquil, September 21, 1822

Having presented the plan and having examined it with all due attention, . . . the first thing to understand is that the miserable, barbarous, politically irrational and unjustifiable condition of the slaves cannot exist in a Republican Government that is truly just and humanitarian; second, that the rights of owners are not harmed; and third, above all, that in no case will the public tranquility be exposed and compromised; it is found that the said plan . . . is worthy of the approval of His Excellency the Lord Liberator-President . . . , with the following declarations. . . .

6th item: that the 4th article of Chapter 3 will not compromise a male or female slave who after having begun to contribute [to the freedom fund], it turns out to be physically impossible to continue because of an illness or injury that overwhelms them; for these there should be the option for freedom even if they cannot continue their contribution, since they may lean on the good will of their companions who are pledged to the general relief. . . .

Dr. Joaquín Salazar

28

Slavery after Independence, Peru

1821

After the independence of Spanish continental America, the countries of Peru, Bolivia, Colombia, Venezuela, and Ecuador continued to maintain large populations of slaves. The principal leader of the independence movement of Spanish America, Simón Bolívar, opposed slavery and understood that its survival was contrary to the new nations' ideals. Although he opposed immediate emancipation, he argued that the national governments should commit to emancipationist policies. Thus several of the recently independent states drafted laws for the gradual abolition of slavery. According to the most common of these laws, the "free womb" laws, the children of slaves born after the declaration of independence would be considered free. This was the case, for example, in Chile in 1811 and in the region of Río de la Plata in 1813.

Manuel Lucena Samoral, *Leyes para esclavos: El ordenamiento jurídico sobre la condición, tratamiento, defensa y represión de los esclavos en la colonias de la América española* (Madrid: Fundacións Histórica Tavera, 2000), 1220–21. Translated by John Michael Corley.

Peruvians formally declared independence on July 28, 1821. Soon thereafter, the leader José San Martín issued the Free Womb Law. Landowners and slaveowners intervened, however, to substantially modify the original proposal. A later decree established that freed persons should stay under the control of their mothers' owners until they reached the age of twenty, in the case of women, and twenty-four, in the case of men. The liberty of the individuals affected by the Free Womb Law was delayed by two decades, so that in practice these freed persons continued to be bought and sold as if they were still slaves. Even so, slaves continued to press for liberation. Many slaves managed to buy their freedom, especially after 1840; others successfully pursued legal action against their owners for their emancipation. In 1851, the first Peruvian civil code legally sanctioned the relations between slaves and owners that had already existed in practice. Three years later, in 1854, slavery was abolished in Peru.

General José de San Martín, Decree Declaring Freedom for Children Born of Slaves after July 28

Lima, Peru, August 12, 1821

When humanity has been highly outraged and has had its rights violated for a long time, it is a great act of justice, if not to repay entirely, then at least to give the first steps toward the completion of the most holy of obligations. A numerous portion of our kind has been, up to now, looked upon as a thing to be traded, and subject to the calculations of criminal trafficking; men have bought other men, and have shown no shame in the degradation of the families to whom they belong, in being sold to disparate masters. The institutions of the barbarous centuries, supported over the course of years, have established the right of ownership of men in contravention of the most august of rights that nature has granted. Nevertheless, I am not endeavoring, in one blow, to attack this ancient abuse; the very years that have sanctioned it must now destroy it; but I would violate my public conscience and my private feelings if I were not to prepare for the coming of this pious reform, thus temporarily gaining the interest of the slaveowners with a vote of reason and of nature. Therefore, I declare the following:

1. All the children of slaves who were or will be born in the Territory of Peru following the 28th of July in the present year in which [Peru] declared its independence, including the states that find them-

selves still occupied by enemy forces, and who belong to the State, shall be free and will enjoy the same rights as the rest of the Citizens of Peru with the modifications that will be expressed in a separate ruling.

2. The certificates of baptism of those born after July 28, 1821 will serve as official documents, showing the restoration of this right. Let this decree be printed, published by proclamation, and circulated.

Given in Lima, the 12th of August of 1821, the second year of the freedom of Peru.
[by General José de] San Martín.
Bernardo Monteagudo

"Just Evaluation" Case of Joana Monica, Lima, Peru, 1826

Peru's proclamation of independence inaugurated a turbulent period in the legal status of slavery. The government instituted a variety of changes in order to recruit new soldiers for the wars against Spain until 1824, when the Spanish forces were finally defeated. As long as the Peruvian army needed troops, the government of the recently independent country facilitated the emancipation of the slaves. Slaveowners, however, never stopped opposing these measures.

In March 1824, Bolívar promulgated another law, which allowed slaves to change owners at will. This measure was widely opposed by slaveowners, who feared losing slaves, particularly since the end of the slave trade made it increasingly difficult to replace them.

Slaves took advantage of the emancipationist measures. In the case of variación de domínio *[change of control], they forced their sale to new owners, prevented their being sold to distant regions, and obtained reductions in their price. Through these actions, they managed to broaden their chances of achieving freedom, and such strategies clearly played an important role in the disintegration of slavery in Peru.*

Juana Monica initiated in 1826 a trial in order to guarantee her sale "at just price." She complained about her master's abuses and founded

Case summary and document translation by Carlos Aguírre, "Working the System: Black Slaves and the Courts in Lima, Peru, 1821–1854," in Darlene Clark Hine and Jacqueline McLeod, eds., *Crossing Boundaries: Comparative History of Black People in Diaspora* (Bloomington: Indiana University Press, 1999), 213–14.

her case upon: "the prerogatives slaves have for seeking a buyer at his/her satisfaction. . . . I want to withdraw from this hostile and inhumane rule. [My master didn't want me to continue to demand my freedom, and attempted to] send me in a ship to a site in which distance will put my freedom to silence, treating me not as a rational being but as a beast incapable of reason. . . . If our liberal constitutions and a wise decree by Your Excellence the liberator [Bolívar] have some value against the stingy enactments of the Spanish law, it is the liberty that every human being has to avoid being a serf, and the slave to search for a master, leaving behind a tyrannical power."

Juana Monica was ill. Her owner priced her at 300 pesos, the same price he had paid for her initially. When she was allowed to seek a buyer, nobody was willing to pay that price. The slave argued that: "This is a conflict that I don't know how to solve. If I go back to my house, I will become a victim of my master's furies . . . and if I go to a different place, I will experience disavowal because nobody wants ill people in their houses."

The master agreed to sell her for 200 pesos, but it did not work. The slave insisted in being appraised by the judge. Finally she was valued at 100 pesos. The *variación de domínio* was then granted.

29

DON GERÓNIMO VALDÉS

Regulations concerning Slaves Destined for Cuba

November 14, 1842

As slavery waned in most of Spanish America, it expanded dramatically in the Caribbean island colonies of Cuba and Puerto Rico. Spain, seeking to expand the plantation economy, forcibly transported hundreds of thousands of slaves from Africa, transforming Cuba into one of the most important slave societies in all the Americas.

Manuel Lucena Samoral, *Leyes para esclavos: El ordenamiento jurídico sobre la condición, tratamiento, defensa y represión de los esclavos en la colonias de la América española* (Madrid: Fundacións Histórica Tavera, 2000), 1258–64. Translated by John Michael Corley.

The Regulations concerning Slaves Destined for Cuba, consisting of forty-eight articles, was published in November 1842 as one of the annexes of the Governor General's Proclamation for the Governance and Policing of the Island of Cuba. Although based on the regulations for Puerto Rico, the Cuban legislation instituted harsher measures—for example, increasing daily working hours and eliminating the slaveowners' obligation to feed their slaves' children.

Article 32. Courts may require slave owners to sell their slaves . . . when owners abuse, mistreat, or commit inhumane or unreasonable excesses against the slaves. The price in these cases is to be based upon each individual's skills . . . or by a third party in case of a disagreement; but if there is a buyer who wants to take them without evaluation for the price that the owner demands, the court will not be able to impede the sale in his favor.

Article 33. When owners sell their slaves because it suits them, that is to say voluntarily, they will be at liberty to do so for the price they choose, according to the greater or lesser value of the slaves.

Article 34. No slave owner will be allowed to oppose the *coartación* of his slaves, provided that they are shown to be valued at a price of at least fifty pesos.

Article 35. Slaves under *coartación* cannot be sold for a higher price than that which had been fixed on them at the evaluation, and this condition will pass from buyer to buyer. Nevertheless, if the slave wishes to be sold against his owner's wishes, without any just reason for it, or gives an opportunity [*dar margen para*] with his bad attitude to proceed with the transfer, the owner will be able to raise the price of the *coartación* tax and the rights of the deed that sets the terms of sale.

Article 36. As the condition of *coartación* is limited to an individual, the children of the mothers under *coartación* will not enjoy its benefit and thus may be sold like all the other slaves.

Article 37. Owners will give freedom to slaves as soon as they receive the price of their value, provided that it is acquired legitimately; this price—in the case when there is no agreement among the interested parties—will either be determined by . . . the owner . . . or, failing that, the court, or another will be chosen by the Procurator General Trustee representing the slave, and a third party, chosen by the said court, in case of disagreement. . . .

Don Gerónimo Valdés, President, Governor and Captain General. Printed by the Government and the Captaincy General for His Majesty, Havana

30

TOMASA JIMÉNEZ ET AL.

Spanish Slaves' Petition for Freedom, Madrid

March 29, 1836

Some slaves, especially those in urban areas, were aware of their rights and pressured authorities to uphold them. This was the case with a group of Spanish slaves who petitioned for their liberty in 1836, arguing that they were ill-treated by their owners. The Sección de Índias del Consejo Real *(Indian Section of the Royal Council) sent the recommendation below to Queen Isabel II, who ordered colonial authorities to immediately free all slaves that reached Spain. Although there were very few slaves in the mother country, the decree had an important effect: The efforts of the slaves brought about the abolition of slavery in Spain.*

Most excellent Lord,

Tomasa Jiménez, María Antonia García and Tomás Bayanza, all slaves belonging to different owners and living on this peninsula, have come before your Majesty the Queen Governor asking that they be given their freedom, because they believe themselves to have been treated with extreme cruelty by their masters. Having taken notice that Your Majesty deemed it timely to address such extremism [*extremo*], so that it might be resolved in the most informed manner possible, ordered that the Department of the Indies of the Royal Council consult on the matter . . . , verifying as proven, among other things, that the institution of slavery is looked upon with disfavor in the [Iberian] Peninsula, since for lack of buyers it has not been easy to change owners, as happened in America; that neither was it very suitable for the owners to have slaves there, since on finding themselves badly

---

Manuel Lucena Samoral, *Leyes para esclavos: El ordenamiento jurídico sobre la condición, tratamiento, defensa y represión de los esclavos en la colonias de la América española* (Madrid: Fundacións Histórica Tavera, 2000), 1249–50. Translated by John Michael Corley.

served, the owners were exposed to continuous fines, if the protective laws for this class of individuals were duly and vigorously observed; that the public authority has also been demanding freedom, since slavery is considered repugnant and unbecoming to social mores in the territory of Europe; and finally, in order to avoid the inconveniences that result from the presence of slaves in Europe, it would be suitable to communicate to Your Excellency all of the herein listed powerful reasons, to be ready to try to not issue [entry] passports to the slaves [coming] to the Peninsula. And asking Your Majesty to act on the Department's resolution, sent to Your Majesty for execution as a royal decree, adding at the same time that it is the royal will that those who wish to embark slaves [from the colonies] be obliged to free them once they arrive at the Peninsula.

31
A Bread Seller and Seller of Fodder,
Havana, Cuba
ca. 1851

In this lithograph by an unknown artist, the baker (left) and the seller of fodder (right) are each accompanied by their black assistants, who are likely enslaved. It was not unusual for urban slaves like these to make deliveries and collect payments independently, turning over a portion of their earnings to their masters. Through such participation in cash economies it was possible for some urban slaves to earn enough money to purchase their own freedom or that of their loved ones. The Spanish practice of coartación *allowed slaves and masters to agree upon a purchase price and for slaves to pay for their freedom in installments.* Coartación *led to a relatively high rate of manumission in Spanish America, though this trend was curtailed somewhat when Cuba and other colonies embraced the plantation system.*

32

Royal Order, Madrid

August 2, 1861

In addition to abolishing slavery in Spain, the 1836 decree (see Document 30) created new avenues to freedom for slaves living in the Spanish Empire. The law left ambiguous the status of slaves who traveled from Spain to the Antilles, either voluntarily or against their will. In 1861, O'Donnell, Lord Governor Captain General of the island of Puerto Rico, raised this question based on the case of former slave Rufino.

Royal Order Declaring That the Slaves Who Have Arrived in the Iberian Peninsula, Having Been Emancipated, Will Not Lose Their New Condition If They Return to the Spanish Slave Colonies

[From] The Ministry of War and Foreign Affairs.

Most Excellent Lord,

I have given... the Queen (may God protect her) thoughtful remarks concerning the sale to Havana of one Rufino, who has resided several years in the [Iberian] Peninsula, for which reason he has begged for a declaration explaining the royal decree of March 29, 1836, referring to the condition by which slaves from the Antilles can be brought to the Peninsula. Your Majesty, having been informed, has agreed to resolve, in conformance with the decision of July 8 [1836], which was passed by the Council of State in plenary session, to the effect that, according to the Royal Decree, slaves who come to Spain from this island [Puerto Rico] and from Cuba should be considered emancipated from their owners, unless they are considered indispensable or unless the slave consents to [remaining enslaved]; that the right of freedom which is conceded to the said slaves by the aforesaid resolution of March 29, 1836, is not by nature revocable, acquiring its effective permanence in the mother country, whether or not there be

---

Manuel Lucena Samoral, *Leyes para esclavos: El ordenamiento jurídico sobre la condición, tratamiento, defensa y represión de los esclavos en la colonias de la América española* (Madrid: Fundacións Histórica Tavera, 2000), 1293. Translated by John Michael Corley.

another act confirming it; and that, for the same reason, [they may] keep their quality as free men, even when they return to a country where slavery is found to be authorized by the [local] laws. By the Royal Decree I call this to Your Excellency's attention, it being at the same time the will of Your Majesty that this resolution be published in the official newspapers of this island and of Cuba, to whose Governor Captain General [will] be sent the notification of it on this date, so that all interested parties [may] be informed, and well supplied everywhere with the information.

May God keep Your Excellency safe for many years.

O'Donnell. Lord Governor Captain General of the island of Puerto Rico.

33

SPANISH CROWN

Law for the Suppression of Slavery and Patronage [in Cuba], Madrid

February 13, 1880

Following many years of war between Cuban independence fighters and Spain, the Spanish "Free Womb" Moret Law of 1871, the establishment of the Spanish Republic in 1873, and Puerto Rican emancipation that same year, the new liberal Spanish government appointed a commission to formulate an emancipation program for Cuba. The commission, which included important shareholders, settled on a gradualist approach: In the year of promulgation, all slaves over fifty-five years of age would be liberated; by 1880, all those over fifty years of age; in 1882, those over forty-five, and so on until 1890, when the remainder would be freed. This policy became law on February 13, 1880, as the Patronato Law. We have translated the words patronos *as "patrons,"* patrocinados *as "clients," and* patronato *as "patronage."*

Enrique Pérez-Cisneros, *La abolición de la esclavitud en Cuba* (San José, Costa Rica: Litografía e Imprenta LIL, 1987), 137–43. Translated by John Michael Corley.

Don Alfonso XII, by the grace of God constitutional King of Spain, to all who are present to see and understand, Know [ye]: That the Courts have decreed and sanctioned us to the following:

Article 1. The state of slavery will cease on the island of Cuba, in accord with the prescriptions of the present law.

Article 2. The individuals who, without violating the law of July 4, 1870, found themselves as slaves in the final census of 1871 and continue in servitude at the promulgation of that law, will remain under the patronage of their owners for the period there established. The patronage will be transmittable by every known legal means, [yet] without transferring the minor children of twelve years of age, and those of the father and mother respectively to the new patron.

In no case shall there be any separation of the individuals that constitute a family, no matter what their origin.

Article 3. The patron will retain the right to use the people of his patronage for work and represent them in all civil and judicial acts in accord with the laws.

Article 4. These will be the obligations of the patrons:

§1. Maintain the clients. . . .

§3. Help them in their illnesses.

§4. Pay [them] for their work with a monthly stipend, as specified in this law.

§5. Give the minors a primary education and training necessary for the exercise of a skill, a position, or useful occupation.

§6. Feed, clothe and help in their illnesses any children of the clients who are in infancy or in puberty, born before and after the patronage, with the ability to take advantage of their labor without payment [of wages].

Article 5. Upon the publication of this law a certificate will be given to the clients, in such form as the rules determine, making evident in it the sum of the rights and obligations of this new condition. . . .

Article 7. The patronage will cease:

§1. By [the] extinction, by means of the order of the gradual ages of the clients, from old to young, in the form determined in article 8, so as to conclude definitely eight years after the publication of this law.

§2. By mutual agreement of the patron and the client, without outside intervention, except for the parents, if known, and in the absence of the respective local laws, when it is a matter of minors under twenty years of age, this age being determined in the manner expressed in Article 13.

§3. By renunciation by the patron, except if the clients are minors, sexagenarians, or were sick or disabled.

§4. By payment for the servants, by means of giving to the patron a sum of 30 to 50 annual pesos, according to the sex, age, and circumstances of the client, based upon the time remaining of the first five years of the patronage and at the mid term of the remaining three years.

§5. By means of any of the causes for manumission established in the civil and penal laws, or for the failure of the patron in the obligations imposed on him by Article 4. . . .

Article 11. The individuals who are [in the transitional state of] *coartación* upon the publication of this law will remain in their new condition as clients with the rights acquired by the *coartación.* Furthermore, they will be able to use the benefit assigned in Article 7, section 4, giving their patrons the difference between the amount they have already paid and that which corresponds to the reimbursement for [or payment for services]. . . .

Article 14. Patrons will not be able to impose corporal punishment, as prohibited by the second paragraph of Article 21 of the Law of July 4, 1870, even under the pretext of maintaining the work regime on the farm. Nevertheless, they will have the coercive and disciplinary facilities that order requires, which are contained in the rules necessary to assure the work and the job needed by that facility. Also, patrons will be able to reduce the monthly stipends proportionate to the lack of work of the employee [*retribuido*], according to the conditions and in the manner that the law affixes.

Article 15. In each province a Committee will be formed, presided over by the Governor and, in his absence, by the President of the Provincial Council, composed of a provincial Deputy, the Judge in the first instance, the Fiscal Officer [*Promotor fiscal*], the District Attorney of the capital and two taxpayers [*contribuyentes*], one of whom will be the patron. At the discretion of the Governors and with the prior approval of the Governor General, local Committees will be formed in the city offices where they will convene, presided over by the Mayor, and composed of the District Attorney, one of the major taxpayers, and two honored neighbors. These Committees and the fiscal Ministry will be alert to the exact compliance with this law, and they will have, in addition, the same powers [*atribuciones*] conferred by the law.

Article 16. The clients will be subject to the ordinary Tribunals for crimes and failures, debts for which they were responsible, in accord with the penal code, with the exception of rebellion, sedition, illegal offense [*atentado*] and public disorder, which will be judged under a military court. Nevertheless, patrons will have access to the governing Authority [*Autoridad governativa*] loaned to them for their help against the clients who violate the work rules; if their actions are insufficient to impede [the disorder], the patron will be . . . able to . . . force the client to work on public works for the period set by law, . . . within the time remaining until the end of the patronage. If the client repeats an offense after having been placed into the said service, or abandons it or gravely disturbs order in the same manner the Governor General can order . . . that [the client] be sent to the Spanish islands of the African coast, where he will remain subject to the vigilance fixed by the law. . . .

Article 18. All laws, regulations and decrees in opposition to this law are hereby nullified, without prejudice to the rights acquired already by the slaves and freedmen, in conformity with the law of July 4, 1870, in everything not expressly altered by the above articles. . . .

Given in the Palace. I, the King [*Yo el Rey*]. The Ministry of the Exterior, José Elduayen.

In 1885, there was almost no resistance to the idea of final abolition, which in this case meant the end of patronato. *Since the vast majority of* patrocinados *had already obtained their liberty, there was less concern with the possible effects of the measure. At the same time, many considered the intermediary labor system to be problematic. In August 1886, after meeting with representatives of Cuban landowners, the Spanish courts abolished the* patronato *system. From then on, landowners turned their attention to new ways of increasing the labor supply, such as through encouraging large-scale immigration.*

Thus ended the long process of abolition of slavery in Cuba. A new phase of history began: that of the effective social integration of Afrodescendants into Cuban society.

4

Portugal and Brazil

34

PORTUGUESE CROWN

Ordinances and Laws of the Kingdom of Portugal Compiled by Mandate of the Very High Catholic and Powerful King Philip (Ordenações Filipinas)

1603

In contrast with earlier Portuguese law, which addressed slavery in the sections on ecclesiastical persons and goods, the Ordenações Filipinas treated slavery primarily as a commercial practice. This was the first legislation to specifically mention African slaves, as opposed to Moors (who had been captured in the medieval wars between Muslims and Christians over the control of Portuguese territory).

Book IV, Chapter XI. That No One Be Restrained against Their Will from Selling Their Inheritance and Possessions

Each person can sell their possessions to whomever they wish and for the best price they can get, and will not be obliged to sell them to their brother, nor to another relative, nor can they demand the equivalent. In favor of liberty many things are granted against the general rules: if some person owns a captured Moor, for which a request is

Candido Mendes de Almeida, ed., *Ordenações Filipinas* (Lisbon: Fundação Calouste Gulbenkian, 1985). Translated by Mark William Lutes.

made in the case of a need to exchange him for some Christian held captive in the land of the Moors, then if there is a need to pay for and liberate that Moor, we hold that the person who owns this Moor is obliged to sell him and thus be constrained by Law.

Book IV, Chapter LXIII. Of Donations and Emancipation That Can Be Revoked Because of Ingratitude

Donations pure and simple made without any past, present or future condition or cause, either made with the consent of those doing it and acceptance of those to which it is done, or of a notary public or person who by Law can accept in their name, are thus firm and final, such that at no time can they be revoked. However, if those for whom this was done were ungrateful to those who did it, they have cause to revoke these donations as a result of the ingratitude. And the causes are as follows:

1—The first cause is if the beneficiary spoke to the donor, whether in his presence or absence, some serious insult, which causes shame to the donor. . . .

2—The second cause is if the recipient injured the donor with a stick, stone, or iron, or laid a hand on him . . . with the intention to injure or dishonor. . . .

5—The fifth cause is when the beneficiary promises to the donor, in return for making the donation, to give something or fulfill some commitment, which was not given or fulfilled as promised. . . .

7—If someone manumits their slave, freeing him from all servitude and, after being freed, he commits some personal ingratitude against the person who freed him, in their presence or absence . . . this patron can revoke the liberty given to the manumitted person, and reduce him to his previous servitude. . . .

35

PORTUGUESE CROWN

Law of December 24, 1734

Starting in the early eighteenth century, mining by slaves flourished in the Minas Gerais region of southeastern Brazil. Through urban commercial activity and mining—an occupation in which slaves might find valuable stones or could contribute to state control over a lucrative enterprise—many slaves achieved freedom. As a result, in the second half of the century, the population of free people of African descent was ten times greater in Minas Gerais than in many other slave societies, such as Jamaica or the southern United States.

I hereby let it be known that, as the diamond mines that are found in my dominion belong to me, just as do all mines of metals, and I can reserve of them what I find, . . . I declare that in the lands from which diamonds are extracted, . . . those of a weight of twenty carats or more are reserved for my Treasury; and the persons who find or extract will present them within thirty days. . . .

And for those diamonds discovered and delivered by any slave, he will be freed and a letter of emancipation will be given in my name; . . . and to their master will be given for the value of the slave 400$000 *réis.* . . . And if presented by a free man he will be given the same 400$000 *réis.* And all the diamonds weighing twenty carats or more, which are found from this time forward and which are not presented in this manner and are thus lost to my Treasury—no matter whose hand in which they are found or who reports them—when the accusation is made and the diamond is collected, a reward of 400$000 *réis* will be given to the accuser from my Treasury alone. And if the accuser is a slave he will be given liberty and his master given 400$000 *réis* for his value, except in the case where the slave accuses his own master, in which case the slave will be freed and given 200$000 *réis*—both after judgment of the accusation—and the master

Silvia Lara, *Legislação sobre escravos africanos na América Portuguesa* (Madrid: Fundación Histórica Tavera, 2000), 291–93. Translated by Mark William Lutes.

will not receive anything for the value of the slave but will incur the penalties set out below.

And similarly, whoever having taken or found a diamond of twenty carats or more, smuggles it without declaring it and delivering it in the manner described, can be accused, and will, along with losing the diamond or its value, incur the penalties against those who smuggle gold; if a slave, he will be condemned to the lash and forced labor for his entire life. . . .

Issued in Lisbon, December 24, 1734. King.

36

The Coartação *of Rosa Gonçalves da Fonseca, Minas Gerais, Brazil*

1769–1770

Coartação—*equivalent to the Spanish* coartación, *a slave's purchase of freedom through installment payments as negotiated with the master— was rare in most of Brazil but widely adopted in Minas Gerais, where mining work allowed slaves to participate in urban life and the cash economy. The masters' need to minimize expenses for the day-to-day maintenance of their slaves made* coartação *attractive to them. Coartação was commonly accorded to slaves who had previously complied with certain conditions, such as serving the master (or his heirs) for a fixed number of years. Slaves only received the letter of emancipation at the moment they paid the final installment, which meant that there was a period when the slave under* coartação *was in legal terms neither slave nor free.*

The precarious nature of the contracts and agreements involved in the process of coartação *created many conflicts between masters and slaves. In the following case, freed slave Rosa Gonçalves da Fonseca petitioned*

National Library (Rio de Janeiro), Manuscript Section, 18, 3, 2 doc. 148–149. Also cited in Laura de Mello e Souza, "Coartação: Problemática e episódios referentes a Minas Gerais no século XVIII," in Maria Beatriz Nizza da Silva, *Brasil: Colonização e escravidão* (Rio de Janeiro: Nova Fronteira, 2000), 288. Translated by Mark William Lutes.

*the governor for the freedom of her three daughters, born while she was
still paying installments toward her freedom.*

*In 1769, the freed slave sent a petition to the local authorities, asking
that her three daughters be considered free. Francisco Fonseca, widower
of Rosa's former owner Úrsula Gonçalves, responded as follows.*

**Francisco Fonseca, Response by Widower of Former Owner
Úrsula Gonçalves to Suit by Rosa Gonçalves da Fonseca, 1769**

Honorable External Judge,
   The present request that Rosa Gonçalves da Fonseca has made to
[the governor], with the intention that this would lead you to order
that her daughters be delivered to her, on the grounds that both are
free, is found to be devoid of justice; . . . because the document of *coartamento* dated January 27, 1755 states that the said Rosa was
coartada . . . with five *quartos* of gold, whose *coartamento* would begin
after four years [i.e., she would continue working as a slave for four
years], . . . and then the three years of the *coartamento* would start to
pass [i.e., she would be free but have three additional years in which
to pay her final installments]. Before this term expired the said Rosa
Gonçalves da Fonseca was always the slave of Úrsula Gonçalves. . . .
   The supplicant can have no doubt that the daughters of the said
Rosa Gonçalves are my slaves, as shown by the certificates, . . .
because they state that Antonia and Clemência, daughters of the said
D. Rosa, were baptized on respectively March 5, 1756 and November
13, 1757, both of them being born during that four years while their
mother was a slave, and thus have the same status, because clearly in
terms of liberty children follow the nature and condition of their
mother; . . . and with respect to the other daughter named Josefa, she
is also a slave, because having been baptized on February 11, 1759, as
stated on the certificate, she was born within three years of the *coartamento* which was only finalized in 1761.
   And there can be no doubt that children born within the period of
coartamento are slaves, because under the law, every time that some
slave is under that condition, . . . while the condition is not terminated,
the children born to the said slave are also slaves. . . .
   Thus since the said Josefa was born within the three years of *coartamento* of her mother Rosa, the woman is certainly a slave, just as are
the other two daughters Antonia and Clemência, . . . for these reasons
they should not be delivered to the said Rosa Gonçalves, being—as

they are—my slaves, over whom I always had ownership, and I should not be deprived of this.

Francisco Ferreira dos Santos, Judge's Opinion Submitted to the Governor, 1770

Your Excellency the Count of Valadares,
  The petition of Rosa Gonçalves da Fonseca cannot be granted, because she was a slave at the time she gave birth to Antonia and Clemência; which is proven by the document of her *coartamento* and the baptismal certificates of her two daughters Antonia and Clemência. And without much controversy, it seems to me, that Francisco da Fonseca is entitled to have as his own the said daughters of Rosa Gonçalves because they are his slaves and have been so, long before the awarding of the *coartamento* of Rosa Gonçalves, thus it appears to me that Francisco da Fonseca should retain his ownership. . . .
  Your Excellency will determine what is best.

[It is not known whether the governor followed the judge's recommendation. Since neither this opinion nor later correspondence mention Josefa, the judge might already have ruled that she should be considered free.]

37

PORTUGUESE CROWN

Law of Liberty

June 6, 1755

Sixteenth-century Portuguese colonists used indigenous people as laborers extensively in Brazil. Indigenous slavery began to decline in the seventeenth century, partly due to the decimation of the Indians through disease and warfare, but also due to their flight to the continental interior.

Antonio Delgado da Silva, *Collecção da legislação portugueza desde a ultima compilação das ordenaços*, 6 vols. (Lisbon: Maigrense, 1825), 1:369–75. Translated by Mark William Lutes.

*With the support of the Catholic Church, which sought to convert indige-
nous peoples to Christianity, the Portuguese crown passed laws in 1609
and 1680 that proclaimed indigenous people free, regardless of how they
had become enslaved. By 1650, the number of African slaves had sur-
passed the number of indigenous slaves. Even so, Portuguese colonists
continued to illegally enslave indigenous people in more isolated regions
of South America. In the second half of the eighteenth century, the Portuguese government sought to modernize society by adopting mercantilist
and centralizing policies similar to those of France and England. Portugal also took measures to strengthen the central authority—for example,
by expelling the powerful Jesuit religious order in 1767. Amidst these profound political and economic changes, the crown issued the* Lei da Liberdade *(Law of Liberty).*

. . . I hereby let it be known . . . that I decided to find out the true
causes of the fact that since the discovery of Grão-Pará and Maranhão,
the Indians of that State have not only failed to multiply, and become
civilized to date, . . . but, on the contrary, all the Indians that came
from the Hinterlands to the Villages . . . have been always disappear-
ing, so that there are very few settlements, or residents in them; and
these few still live in such great misery that, rather than inviting and
stimulating the other barbarian Indians to imitate them, they serve as
a scandal . . . encouraging others to remain in their wild dwellings with
lamentable prejudice to the salvation of their souls and grave harm to
that State. . . .

It is generally agreed that the cause that has produced such perni-
cious effects is that . . . the Indians weren't efficient in supporting
themselves in their freedom, which was declared in their favor by the
Supreme Pontiffs, and by my predecessor Kings; . . . the provisions of
these Laws have always been undermined by the greed of private
interests, until, becoming acquainted and experienced with these
facts, The King, my Lord and Grandfather, in 1680 . . . established the
Law whose content is as follows:

> I hereby let it be known . . . that . . . the unjust captivity to which the
> residents of the State of Maranhão, through illicit means, have
> reduced its Indians, and of the grave damage, excesses and offences
> to God, that they have committed to this end, enact a Law . . . which
> prohibits this captivity, excepting four cases which in law were just
> and legitimate: when they were taken in a just war, which the Por-
> tuguese pursued, respecting the circumstances declared in the said

Law; or when they prevent Preaching of the Gospel; or when they were tied up and bound so as to be cannibalized; or when they were taken captive by other Indians, who had taken them in a just war, the justice of which being examined pursuant to the said Law. And because this prescription has not been effective, . . . I order that from this point forward no Indian can be taken captive in the said State under any circumstances, not even under the exceptions in the said Laws. . . . Lisbon, April 1, 1680.

And because time has made more notorious and obvious the very just causes, for which this Law was established to restore the Indians to their old and natural liberty, . . . I consider it appropriate . . . to repeal . . . all the Laws, Regulations, Resolutions and orders, which . . . until the present day have permitted . . . the enslavement of the said Indians. . . .

The King.

38

The Freedom Suit of the Slave Liberata, Desterro, Santa Catarina

1813

Brazilian slaves had sued their masters for freedom since the sixteenth or seventeenth century, but freedom suits became an especially important means by which slaves sought emancipation in the nineteenth century. One common type of freedom suit arose when a master or his heirs rescinded a slave's letter of emancipation. Others grew out of failed manumission negotiations. Slaves sued for freedom on the basis of their arrival in Brazil after the abolition of the slave trade (in 1831 or, definitively, 1850), or they accused their masters of mistreatment.

Process 1337, stack 214, Desterro. Court of Appeal, National Archive of Rio de Janeiro. Summarized and quoted in Keila Grinberg, *Liberata, a lei da ambiguidade — as ações de liberdade da Corte de Apelação do Rio de Janeiro no século XIX* (Rio de Janeiro: Relume Dumará, 1994), 15–32. Translated by Mark William Lutes.

Around 1790, José Vieira Rebello, resident of Enseada das Garoupas, near the city of Desterro (now Florianópolis) in the south of Brazil, purchased a ten-year-old slave, Liberata, who was born in Brazil. Over the following years, Rebello seduced Liberata, promising to free her if she consented to sexual relations with him.

Liberata became his lover. Three years later, she gave birth to their first son, whom her master recognized as his child. Persecuted by her master's wife and children because of the illicit relations, Liberata began to pressure her master to speed up her manumission. She again became pregnant by Rebello. This time, under pressure from his family, Rebello refused to baptize the child as his own. To escape punishment from the family, Liberata had to declare that the newborn child was a slave. From then on, she became more emphatic in demanding her freedom.

During this same period, Anna Vieira, the single, legitimate daughter of her master, had several babies, at least one of whom was fathered by a black slave of the house. All were killed as newborns: One was suffocated in Anna's bedroom, another was killed by Anna and Rebello and buried under a guava tree nearby, another had been thrown into the ocean, and yet another was buried near a spring on the farm. After one of these babies' deaths, Liberata reproached her master, who told her that "it was better to keep quiet, because they didn't want anybody to know about this." Having witnessed all these crimes, Liberata was regularly threatened by Anna Vieira and later by Rebello, too.

In mid-1812, Liberata began a relationship with Francisco José, of mixed race, whom she intended to marry as soon as she obtained her freedom. After trying unsuccessfully to purchase Liberata's freedom, José asked the local parish priest, Agostinho Mendes dos Reis, to intercede with Rebello to convince him to accept the amount of 115,200 réis in exchange for Liberata's freedom. Rebello wouldn't agree to the marriage or to setting her free.

Francisco José, Petition to the Municipal Judge of Desterro, July 1813

Says Liberata, a mixed-race slave woman, of José Vieira Rebello, . . . that she is a supplicant as a miserable and destitute person, with no one to commiserate with her aside from the sacred laws of His Royal Highness, and the justices of the same sovereign Lord, and implores on her knees for all the due license by this first voice to be able to, in his name, make known to the Justice the torments of her captivity, the mistreatment she has suffered day after day without respite, without access to the means to complain through her guardian, having been in private captivity, guarded, and unable to obtain the means to be heard.

The petition detailed the promises of liberty made by José Vieira Rebello, described the children that Liberata had, and requested her emancipation "in conformity with the sacred laws." As soon as the lawsuit was received, Francisco José was appointed trustee; Liberata went to live with him. Rebello was summoned to testify.

Rebello was summoned to court twice as a defendant and was threatened with arrest for failure to appear. Instead of appearing at the Desterro court, he illegally traded "that mulatta who didn't even come to the house anymore" for a slave belonging to his stepson, Floriano José Marques, who then became Liberata's master. Since it was not Marques who had promised to free Liberata, Rebello apparently hoped to moot Liberata's claim.

From September 1813 to the middle of 1814, Floriano José Marques and Francisco José each sent a series of petitions to the Desterro judge. Marques argued that Liberata should be sent back to his custody since the freedom lawsuit could no longer proceed, and Francisco José denounced the illegality of the exchange of slaves and argued that the court case should proceed.

Finally, Francisco José revealed to the judge what he claimed was the true reason Rebello did not want to appear as defendant in the case: the murders of his grandchildren, the babies of Anna Vieira. Summoned to court in July 1814, Liberata testified: "I hadn't spoken before out of fear, but the way and the art with which [Rebello] hid his crimes always disturbed my peace, and my conscience."

One month later, in a surprising turn of events, Francisco José released Liberata from his trusteeship, saying he didn't "need her for anything, and that she is in fact doing him a favor by leaving." A few days later, he petitioned the Desterro judge to name another trustee for Liberata. Meanwhile, Liberata accepted Floriano Marques's unconditional offer of freedom. At the end of October 1814, the lawsuit was withdrawn.

But the story was not over.

In October 1835, Liberata's youngest children, José and Joaquina, asked the Desterro judge for protection so they could initiate their own freedom lawsuits. Represented in court by trustee João José Câmara, they were fighting an attempt to reenslave them by Joaquina Rosa Tavares, the widow of Major Antônio Luís de Andrade, in whose house they lived.

The children told the following story: Floriano Marques had only manumitted Liberata in exchange for lands surreptitiously offered by José

Vieira Rebello. The arrangement was that Liberata would be free, Rebello would be saved from accusations of crime, and Marques would be compensated. This was why Liberata's lawsuit had been withdrawn two decades earlier. But there had been no happy ending for Liberata's youngest children, from her marriage with José. They felt abandoned: "Their Father did not love them because he hadn't raised them, their Patron José Vieira [Rebello] hated them, and the Mother, even if she loved them, intended to get [re-]married. . . ." In keeping with local custom, Liberata's new husband would not support his stepchildren.

José and Joaquina were sent by the Orphan Court to Major Antônio Luís de Andrade, for him to raise and educate, and to teach the tailoring trade to José. But the major did something else entirely. He erased Liberata's name from the children's baptism certificates, thereby destroying the proof of their liberty. After his death, his widow wanted to include them in the estate as slaves. José and Joaquina took advantage of the occasion to request their liberty, for fear of being sold suddenly "and perhaps transported to a place where they would no longer have any type of recourse."

Joaquina Rosa Tavares argued that removing the slaves would violate her property rights. But the argument of José and Joaquina's lawyer was more convincing: showing that there was no document proving ownership of the two by Major Antônio Luís de Andrade, he asserted that the widow Joaquina Tavares had no legal basis for claiming property rights. He cited Paragraph 4 of Chapter 11 of the Ordenações Filipinas, according to which "the arguments in favor of liberty are always stronger," and demanded the liberation of José and Joaquina.

On July 18, 1837, Judge Severo Amorim do Valle handed down a decision that, since Joaquina Tavares had not effectively proven her ownership of José and Joaquina, "the arguments in favor of liberty are stronger than those justifying slavery." At the end of 1838, the Appeals Court of Rio de Janeiro confirmed the decision: José and Joaquina, children of Liberata, were considered "as free as if they had been born from a free womb."

39

JACQUES ARAGO

Iron Mask and Collar
for Punishing Slaves, Brazil

ca. 1817–1820

This image illustrates a punishment inflicted upon slaves, as observed by the Frenchman Jacques Arago during one of his trips to Rio de Janeiro, Brazil, ca. 1817–1820. According to his writings, slaves were "punished in this manner because their misery caused them to eat earth to end their lives." Medical researchers, however, now recognize that eating earth (geophagy) is a response to nutritional deficiencies; it continues to occur under conditions of extreme poverty today. In any case, the device is typical of the brutality and humiliation inflicted upon slaves in many slave societies.

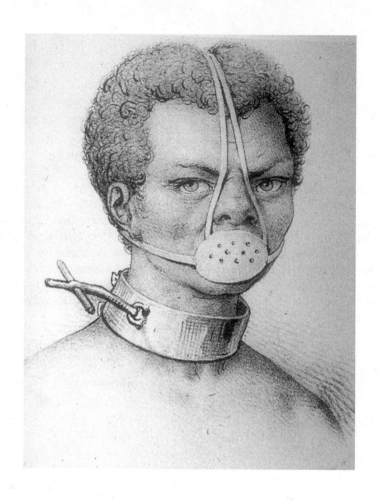

40

Political Constitution of the Empire of Brazil

1824

*The most important legal measure resulting from Brazilian indepen-
dence in 1822 was the drafting of the first constitution, promulgated in
1824. In contrast with the simultaneous independence movements of the
Spanish colonies, which resulted in new republics, independent Brazil
remained politically and economically intertwined with the Portuguese
empire.*

*After independence, though some Brazilians began to call for an end
to the slave trade, neither the trade nor slavery itself was immediately
abolished due to the dependence of the Brazilian economy on slave labor.
Even so, the Brazilian Imperial Constitution set down fundamental
principles for citizenship that directly affected the lives and status of free
blacks.*

Chapter II: Of Brazilian Citizens

Art. 6. Brazilian citizens are:

1. Those born in Brazil, whether born free or liberated, even if
   the father is a foreigner, given that he doesn't reside [in
   Brazil] because of service to his nation.
2. The children of a Brazilian father, and illegitimate children of
   a Brazilian mother, born in a foreign country, who come to
   establish residence in the Empire.
3. The children of a Brazilian father, who is in a foreign country,
   in service to the Empire, even if they do not establish residence in Brazil.
4. All those born in Portugal and its possessions, who, being
   already residents in Brazil at the time of proclamation of independence in the Provinces, where they lived, agreed with it,
   expressly or tacitly, by the continuation of their residence.

500 Anos de Legislação Brasileira, CD-ROM (Brasilia: Senado Federal, 2000). Translated
by Mark William Lutes.

5. Naturalized foreigners, whatever their religion. The law will determine the qualities required to obtain a letter of naturalization.

. . .

Art. 179. The inviolability of the civic and political rights of Brazilian citizens, which is based on liberty, individual security and property, is guaranteed by the Constitution of the Empire. . . .

4. All citizens can be admitted to civil, political or military public positions, with no distinctions made other than their talents and virtues.

41

Legislative Measures against the Slave Trade, Brazil

1831–1850

Newly independent Brazil sought recognition by other nations, in part to ensure that Portugal would not try to reclaim Brazilian territory. Brazil and England signed agreements in 1826 that were based on the old treaties between England and Portugal restricting the slave trade. These agreements led to the Brazilian law of November 7, 1831, which prohibited the transatlantic slave trade. Although this law caused a temporary drop in the importation of Africans, it ended up stimulating a race to purchase slaves within Brazil. The Brazilian government, meanwhile, took no real measures against smuggling: Few cargos were confiscated, and the captured Africans, who were supposed to be sent back to Africa, ended up being re-enslaved. After 1834, Brazil formally labeled them as free Africans, but they were still required to serve the state or private parties. As a result, the importation of Africans resumed on a large scale.

500 Anos de Legislação Brasileira, CD-ROM (Brasilia: Senado Federal, 2000). Translated by Mark William Lutes.

To the present day, the law of 1831 is known as the "law for the English to see" because of its ineffectiveness.

In 1845, the British Parliament passed the Aberdeen Act, legalizing the seizure under any circumstances of any Brazilian ship involved in the black slave trade, including those in Brazilian territorial waters. Five years later, in a context of growing international tension and strong anti-British feeling, the Brazilian government approved Law #581 of 1850. Since the 1850 law overrode the 1831 law without revoking it, it effectively legitimated the entrance of the one million African slaves who had arrived since 1831. Furthermore, slave-trading vessels continued to enter Brazilian waters illegally until 1856.

Law of November 7, 1831

Art. 1. All slaves who enter the territory or ports of Brazil, coming from outside, will be free. Exceptions are:

1. Slaves enrolled in the service of vessels belonging to a country where slavery is permitted, while employed in the service of that vessel.
2. Those escaping from the territory, or the foreign vessel, will be delivered to the masters who claim them, and re-exported to outside of Brazil. . . .

Art. 2. Importers of slaves to Brazil will be subject to the corporal penalty in Art. 179 of the Criminal Code imposed on those who reduce free persons to slavery and will be fined 200$000 per person for each of the slaves imported, along with paying the expenses of re-exporting to any part of Africa; such re-exportation the Government will carry out as soon as possible, contracting the African authorities to give them asylum. The offenders will be held responsible individually and as a group.

Law No. 581, September 4, 1850

Art. 1. Brazilian vessels, found in any part and foreign ones found in the ports, bays, anchorages, or territorial oceans of Brazil, having

---

500 Anos de Legislação Brasileira, CD-ROM (Brasilia: Senado Federal, 2000). Translated by Mark William Lutes.

on board slaves . . . or having unloaded them, will be seized by the authorities or by Brazilian warships and considered importers of slaves.

Those who don't have slaves on board but are found with signs of being used in the slave trade will be seized as well and considered as attempting to import slaves. . . .

Art. 3. Those perpetrators of the crime of importation, or of attempting this importation, are the owner, the captain or master, the pilot and the first mate of the vessel, and the supercargo. Accomplices are: the crew and those who assist with unloading the slaves on Brazilian territory, or who contribute to hiding information from the authorities, or who avoid apprehension at sea, or in the act of disembarking, or being pursued.

Art. 4. The importation of slaves to territory of the Empire will therein be considered piracy, and will be punished by its courts. . . .

Art. 5. The vessels . . . and all the boats used in unloading, hiding or smuggling the slaves, will be sold with all the cargo found on board, and the returns will belong to the parties making the seizure, with one fourth deducted for the informant, if there is one. . . .

Art. 6. All the slaves that were seized will be re-exported by the State to the ports where they originated or to any other point outside the Empire, which appears more appropriate to the Government. . . .

Eusébio de Queiroz Coutinho Mattoso Câmara

42

Battle in the Courts

Until 1850, at least half of the slaves in Brazil's southeastern Paraíba River Valley, where the largest coffee plantations were located, were born in Africa. By 1860, only 20 percent of the slave population was African-born. This is because, along with slaves' natural reproduction, owners in prosperous regions purchased many Brazilian-born slaves from economically depressed areas, such as Pernambuco. These enslaved men and

Freedom Lawsuit at Court of Appeal, box 216, no. 3170. 1866, Barra Mansa, Rio de Janeiro. National Archives, Rio de Janeiro. Translated by Mark William Lutes.

women, born and raised in Brazil, held a memory of slavery, with rights that they refused to give up.

As these recent migrants, torn from their families and forcibly relocated to the Paraíba River Valley, noted the risk to their rights and the worsening of living conditions, many struggled openly against their masters. Some killed their overseers or masters, while others ran away. Still others looked for ways to obtain their freedom. One way was through freedom lawsuits, which increased dramatically, especially in the 1860s. More than half the freedom lawsuits filed in Brazil after 1850 originated in the Paraíba River Valley. Alongside the personal meaning, freedom suits now took on political significance: Each decision in favor of a slave encouraged others to go to court. The cases were tried by abolitionist lawyers, who recruited plantation slaves to sue their masters for their freedom.

Various Slaves, Freedom Lawsuit, Barra Mansa (Paraíba River Valley), Rio de Janeiro, 1866

On April 3, 1855, slaveowner José Pereira Leal wrote letters of emancipation for his slaves, mentioning thirty-one slaves in his will. The letters, which were not delivered to the slaves, specified that they would only receive "the full enjoyment of liberty" after their master's death. In a second will, however, Leal annulled the manumission and declared the letters revoked. In 1866, the slaves began a freedom lawsuit against Leal's heirs.

FÉLIX ANTONIO PEREIRA LIMA, *LAWYER'S STATEMENT CLAIMING HIS CLIENTS' FREEDOM*, 1866

Liberty is a natural right, an absolute, inalienable and invaluable right. . . . Once conceded it can no longer be revoked, and actually there is no human being who can destroy it. By the Imperial Constitution, Article 6, Paragraph 1, the freed person becomes a citizen, enjoys political rights, and can be admitted into civil and military positions. Thus the individual to whom liberty is conceded can no longer return to slavery. By manumission they become a citizen. . . . Certainly the Constitution doesn't allow the freed-person-turned-citizen to return to slavery. . . . It is only possible for this revocation to take place if the recipient of freedom has practiced against the person of the donor some act that shows ingratitude. . . . But . . . to be able to revoke the donation, it is necessary to do so through a competent [judicial] action; while he was living the master did not pursue a court action to revoke the manumission. It is essential to declare in the court the causes of the revocation, and prove it fully. This was not what the donor did in this second will: he limited himself to declaring in it that he had made an earlier will with some letters of emancipation that he had revoked, and nothing more.... There is no doubt, considering what was said, that Oliveira and Irmão, the current holders of those placed under my guardianship, can have no rights over my clients, who have been free since April of 1855.

OLIVEIRA AND IRMÃO, *STATEMENT OF LAWYERS REPRESENTING THE SLAVEHOLDER'S HEIRS*

Oliveira and Irmão, farmers established in this region, appear before Your Worship [the Judge] to complain about the irregular and tumultuous legal process pursued by Dr. Luiz Antonio Vieira as trustee and regarding the alleged emancipations related to certain slaves left by the late José Pereira Leal.... It will not take much to show the inconsistent and impolitic nature of the appointment of Dr. Luiz Antonio Vieira as the trustee of the intended freed persons. Whoever has, as you have, in recent times, lived in this city knows the degree and extent of the ill will that the appointee and all his family bear for the supplicants [heirs of José Pereira Leal] and their relatives.... The zeal or interest for the benefit of liberties never passed through the mind of the appointee who pretends to have such love for a cause with such difficulties and uncertain success. And more a pretext for ostentation, than a sincere desire to sponsor those in his tutelage....

[The slaves' absence for over forty days has already caused financial hardship to the heirs, who] are Brazilians from the patriotic school who think that slavery offends the equality created by God among men and today is maintained by a concurrence of important social considerations. But they also want the favor conceded to liberty to be compatible with the existence of acquired rights—the moral respect that is attributed to the free state of man doesn't extend to the point of undermining in a violent and arbitrary manner the dominion that the master has over his slave....

JUDGE OF BARRA MANSA, *RULING*

I declare free Faustino Benguela, Domingos Moçambique, Francisca, Teresa, Manoel, Joaquim, Quintino, his wife Joaquina, and her children Carolina and Rita, Catarina and her daughter Felicidade, a black woman Maria, João, Silvestre, Josefa, those which are named in the letters of emancipation, as well as the black son of Maria and her recent born son and the others . . . who were born after the death of the donor, in 1858, during which time their mothers were emancipated. I sentence the heirs to relinquish the dominion which they inappropriately exercised over them.

APPEALS COURT, *RULING*, RIO DE JANEIRO, NOVEMBER 3, 1868

[Oliveira and Irmão appealed. The slaves' trustee, for his part, complained that the decision held the date of liberation to be that of the master's death (1858), not the date of the first will and the emancipation letters (1855).]

Upon examination . . . of these documents, the [lower court] judge rendered his judgement . . . proclaiming the individuals mentioned in it free; because . . . for declaration of liberty it matters little the form by which it is conferred, needing only to be revealed in a clear and positive manner the intention to confer it. . . . One cannot raise doubts that the letters of emancipation . . . require nothing more to produce all the effects stipulated in them, principally having been . . . confirmed . . . as true. . . . The said decision was appealed on the grounds that it only considered the children who were born after the death of their parents' benefactor freed; . . . all the children of the slaves born after having had conferred on them conditional liberty would have to be free. Amending therefore the decision appealed in this part, all the slaves mentioned are proclaimed free since the date of their letters, and also all the children born after their mothers had been conceded the said liberty. . . .

Slaves Lino and Lourenço, Freedom Lawsuit, Rio Pardo, Rio Grande do Sul, 1866–1875

This case illustrates a situation that was common in the 1860s, when Brazil was at war with its neighbor Paraguay. A slaveowner, Augusto César de Morais, rented out two slaves, Lino and Lourenço, and some carts to José Teixeira Bastos, a provisioner for the Brazilian army. Bastos, who lived in the extreme south in Rio Pardo at the border with Argentina, supplied food from Argentina to Brazil's Second Army Corps.

Freedom Lawsuit at Court of Appeal, box 3685, no. 13658. 1866, Rio Pardo, Rio Grande do Sul. National Archives, Rio de Janeiro. Translated by Mark William Lutes.

The laws of 1831 and 1850 prohibiting the slave trade made it impossible for anyone to enter Brazil after 1850 as a slave. Therefore, Morais insisted to Bastos that the slaves not be allowed to cross the border between the Brazilian Empire and the Argentine Republic. Bastos, however, was not able to find free peasants to pull the provision carts from Argentina to Corrientes. Upon being informed that slaves in the service of the Brazilian Army could cross the border without problems, Bastos used Lino and Lourenço to do the work. After Bastos returned Lino and Lourenço to Morais, they sued him. On August 12, 1875, the Appeals Court affirmed that the slaves were free.

ANTONIO VICENTE DE SIQUEIRA PEREIRA LEITÃO,
JUDGMENT, RIO PARDO, AUGUST 2, 1874

From the statement of the accused Augusto César de Morais, the testimony of the witnesses, and more in the proceedings, it is proven that the blacks pursuing liberation, Lino and Lourenço, retained by him as slaves, went and stayed some months in the Province of Corrientes, whence they returned to Brazil, without having escaped—this being the exception in Art. 2 of the Law of November 7, 1831 by which masters can reclaim their slaves to slavery.

The right of the accused to recourse, safeguarded for him, against whoever was responsible for those pursuing freedom having left the territory of the Empire, cannot detract from the right, acquired by them, of being reinstated to their natural state of liberty. . . .

Because of this right no one can be the master of another person, because the person who serves as an object of property is not a simple thing, like the irrational animals and inanimate things. Equity demands that the word of the law—all slaves who enter the territory or ports of Brazil, coming from abroad, are free—applies without making distinctions such as those invoked by the accused, that the law is only related to traffic in slaves, that he had not given his consent to the slaves leaving, and having left covered by Brazilian arms, the right of extraterritoriality, as the privilege conceded to diplomatic agents, immunities that cannot by right resume were conceded by the right of the persons to claim property repugnant to natural right; nor also is there the purpose of invoking the constitutional guarantee of property, because its plenitude cannot cover the illicit: one always presumes the best and the most honest. . . .

The law is so clear that it doesn't depend on an authorized interpretation, specific to the Powers of the State; grammar and logic suffice to know that the existing system of legislation is to slowly abolish slavery, and that, if it is not done suddenly, it is to accustom the present generation to abandon the dreadful custom without disruptions, and continue imposing more and more difficult conditions so that the will is reduced to sustain the vice with which it was created, and gradually become resigned to comply with them. . . .

In sum, the intention of the legislature is that the slave who was in a country where slavery is not permitted is free; that even if they come from a country where it is permitted, he is free. Except for escape, because if this were forgiven, the abolition of slavery would be precipitated by the ease of this; and excepting also the case of the slave coming in the service of the vessel, when he is employed in this.

Therefore, the competent letter of emancipation is passed in favor of the said blacks Lino and Lourenço, who I judge and declare free. . . .

MORAIS, *APPEAL*

There is no way one could deduce the slaves to have acquired the condition of freedom by the simple fact of having gone to a territory that no longer knows slavery. The invocation of the Law of November 7, 1831, is groundless, because its Art. 1 does not permit such a broad interpretation and is limited to declaring free all the slaves that enter national territories or ports coming from abroad, with the exception of: 1) slaves working in the service of vessels belonging to a country where slavery is permitted and while employed in the service of said vessels; and 2) those having escaped from foreign territory or vessels, and who for this reason should be returned to the masters who reclaim them or re-exported to outside of Brazil. The laws should always be understood in a legally competent manner. . . . The Law of November 7, 1831, had no other objective but to prohibit bringing slaves into the country; and to this end declared free all those who, being slaves previously, entered here. Not even the Notice #188 of May 20, 1856, could expand the interpretation of the law, stating as it does the intention to liberate all the slaves that leave the Empire. . . .

It would not be possible to forget the lesson of International Law, in accordance with the best authors, in which the space occupied by a foreign army is ruled, for this army and for all the persons accompanying them, by the laws of the country of origin: which would also be the case in passage through neutral territory, since the foreign army, in its stay or passage, enjoys, in the same way that the embassies and sovereign foreigners enjoy the right of extraterritoriality established by modern International Law as a true fiction, supposing that the said persons have not left the territory of their nation. . . . Now, if this is the case in times of peace, with much more reason this would apply in wartime, when the encampment, based on enemy territory, requires that it be considered as the same nation. . . .

The Province of Corrientes, finally, occupied by the 2nd Brazilian Army Corp, from the right bank of the Uruguay River to the bank of the Paraná River, witnessed the entrance in this part of its territory, during the entire period of the war, of Brazilian slaves, who always returned without the authorities of the Republic . . . opposing their leaving in any way, and thus they would enter Brazil and remain in slavery. And the slaves [Lino and Lourenço], along with all these circumstances, were employed in the service of the Army, delivering provisions: consequently, traveling under the Brazilian flag, remaining (wherever they were) not in a foreign country, but in the Empire, and thus not losing the status of slaves.

43

O MOSQUITO

Propaganda against Brazil's Free Womb Law

August 19, 1871

This Brazilian political cartoon shows a blindfolded figure, representing agriculture (Lavoura), threatened by the hand of government, which is lighting the powder keg of the "servile element." It appeared in a satirical newspaper called O Mosquito, published in Rio de Janeiro from 1869 to 1877. Cartoons like this one were very common in Brazil during the 1870s and 1880s, when slaveowners began to fight the government's new gradual-emancipation laws. On the side of abolition were the Brazilian legislature and crown, especially the emperor's daughter, Princess Isabel, who signed the Free Womb Law in 1871 and the Abolition Law in 1888, while her father was out of the country. In fact, the abolition of slavery was one of the main reasons the planters supported a military coup, which overturned the imperial order to form the Republic of Brazil in 1889.

Reprinted by permission of Robert Conrad.

CORTE

Anno   16$000
Semestre   9$000
Trimestre   5$000

PROVINCIAS

Anno   20$000
Semestre   11$000
Trimestre   6$000

REDACÇÃO 70 RUA DOS OURIVES 2º ANDAR

44

BRAZILIAN CROWN

The Free Womb Law (Law 2040)

September 28, 1871

Just as many U.S. slaves had enlisted in the Union army with the hope of achieving freedom during the Civil War, many Brazilian slaves had served as soldiers in the war with Paraguay with the expectation that they would be freed. With the treaty of 1870 between Brazil and Paraguay, the Brazilian government began to address emancipation directly. Brazilian politicians viewed the U.S. abolition experience with horror and planned to carry out emancipation through gradual reform, rather than through a violent revolutionary transformation.

In 1868, a government commission had drafted the legislation later known as the Free Womb Law. The Brazilian legislature debated the proposal throughout the year 1871. Opposing abolition were representatives of the coffee-growing areas of Rio de Janeiro, São Paulo, and Minas Gerais, especially the most prosperous ones located in the Paraíba River Valley, arguing that the proposed law would infringe on property rights. Supporters of the law responded that owners would be compensated.

After four months of tense debate, the Brazilian Congress approved the Free Womb Law, which forged a powerful association between emancipation and the Brazilian imperial government in the eyes of its citizens.

Art. 1.°—The children of the female slaves that may be born in the Empire from the date of this Law shall be considered to be free.

§ 1.°—The said minors shall remain with and be under the dominion of the owners of the mother, who shall be obliged to rear and take care of them until such children have completed the age of 8 years.

On the child of the slave attaining this age, the owner of its mother shall have the option either of receiving from the State the indemnifi-

---

Robert Conrad, *The Destruction of Brazilian Slavery, 1850–1888* (Berkeley: University of California Press, 1972), 305–9.

cation of 600 dollars (*mil réis*) or of making use of services of the minor until he shall have completed the age of 21 years.

In the former event the Government will receive the minor, and will dispose of him in conformity with the provisions of the present Law.

The pecuniary indemnification above fixed shall be paid in Government bonds, bearing interest at 6 percent per annum, which will be considered extinct at the end of 30 years. . . .

§ 2.°—Any one of those minors may ransom himself from the onus of servitude, by means of a previous pecuniary indemnification, offered by himself, or by any other person, to the owner of his mother, calculating the value of his services for the time which shall still remain unexpired to complete the period, should there be no agreement on the quantum of the said indemnification.

§ 3.°—It is also incumbent on owners to rear and bring up the children which the daughters of their female slaves may have while they are serving the same owners.

Such obligation, however, will cease as soon as the service of the mother ceases. Should the latter die within the term of servitude the children may be placed at the disposal of the Government. . . .

§ 6.°—The services of the children of female slaves shall cease to be rendered before the term marked in § 1, if by decision of the Criminal Judge it be known that the owners of the mothers ill-treat the children, inflicting on them severe punishments. . . .

Art. 2.°—The Government may deliver over to associations which they shall have authorized, the children of the slaves that may be born from the date of this Law forward, and given up or abandoned by the owners of said slaves, or taken away by virtue of Article 1, § 6.

§ 1.°—The said associations shall have a right to the gratuitous services of the minors, until they shall have completed the age of 21 years, and may hire out their services, but shall be bound

1st. To rear and take care of the said minors.

2ndly. To save a sum for each of them, out of the amount of wages, which for this purpose is reserved in the respective statutes.

3rdly. To seek to place them in a proper situation when their term of service shall be ended.

Art. 3.°—As many slaves as correspond in value to the annual disposable sum from the emancipation fund shall be freed in each province of the Empire.

§ 1.°—The emancipation fund arises from—

1st. The tax on slaves.

2ndly. General tax on transfer of the slaves as property.

3rdly. The proceeds of 6 lotteries per annum, ... and the tenth part of those which may be granted from this time forth, to be drawn in the capital of the Empire. ...

Art. 4.°—The slave is permitted to form a saving fund from what may come to him through gifts, legacies, and inheritances, and from what, by consent of his owner, he may obtain by his labour and economy. ...

§ 1.°—By the death of the slave half of his savings shall belong to his surviving widow, if there be such, and the other half shall be transmitted to his heirs in conformity with civil law. In default of heirs the savings shall be adjudged to the emancipation fund of which Article III treats.

§ 2.°—The slave who, through his savings, may obtain means to pay his value has a right to freedom. If the indemnification be not fixed by agreement it shall be settled by arbitration. In judicial sales or inventories the price of manumission shall be that of the valuation.

§ 3.°—It is further permitted the slave, in furtherance of his liberty, to contract with a third party the hire of his future services, for a term not exceeding 7 years, by obtaining the consent of his master, and approval of the Judge of the Orphans' Court. ...

§ 5.°—The manumission, with the clause of services during a certain time, shall not become annulled by want of fulfilling the said clause, but the freed man shall be compelled to fulfil, by means of labour in the public establishments, or by contracting for his services with private persons. ...

§ 7.°—In any case of alienation or transfer of slaves, the separation of husband and wife, and children under 12 years of age from father or mother, is prohibited under penalty of annulment. ...

Art. 6.°—The following shall be declared free:

§ 1.°—The slaves belonging to the State, the Government giving them such employment as they may deem fit.

§ 2.°—The slaves given in usufruct to [for use by] the Crown.

§ 3.°—The slaves of unclaimed inheritances.

§ 4.°—The slaves who have been abandoned by their owners. Should these have abandoned the slaves from the latter being invalids they shall be obliged to maintain them, except in case of their own penury, the maintenance being charged by the Judge of the Orphans' Court.

§ 5.°—In general the slaves liberated by virtue of this Law shall be under the inspection of Government during 5 years. They will be

obliged to hire themselves under pain of compulsion; if they lead an idle life they shall be made to work in the public establishments. . . .
Art. 8.°—The Government will order the special registration of all the slaves existing in the Empire to be proceeded with, containing a declaration of name, sex, age, state, aptitude for work, and filiation [names of parents] of each, if such should be known.

. . .

§ 2.°—The slaves who, through the fault or omission of the parties interested, shall not have been registered up to one year after the closing of the register, shall, de facto, be considered as free. . . .

Given at the Palace of Rio de Janeiro, on the 28th September, 1871.
PRINCESS IMPERIAL, REGENT.

45

Just Evaluation of a Slave: The Case of Eubrásia, Campinas, São Paulo

1881–1883

One of the most common disputes occurring after the promulgation of the Free Womb Law involved the slave's price. Although masters could not prevent slaves from purchasing their freedom, they could argue that the price proposed by the slave was too low. These conflicts frequently ended up in the courts. In civil actions like this, the role of the court was to appoint arbitrators who could assess the slave and establish a fair price. With the growth of the abolitionist movement and the greater sympathy throughout society for the cause of slaves, it was common during the 1880s for these cases to settle upon a relatively low price that the slaves were able to pay.

CMU-TJC, 2° OFÍCIO, Arbitramento, 1881; cx R-2, doc. 1686. Joseli Mendonça, "A arena jurídica e a luta pela liberdade," in Lilia M. Schwarcz and Letícia V. de Souza Reis, eds., *Negras imagens—Ensaios sobre cultura e escravidão no Brasil* (São Paulo, EDUSP/ Estação Ciência, 1996), 117–37. Translated by Mark William Lutes.

Early in 1881, the slave Eubrásia deposited the amount of 300,000 réis (about one-third the purchase price of an adult male slave) with the tax collection office for the city of Campinas, to purchase her freedom. In December of the same year, she presented to the court savings of 500,000 réis for a total of 800,000 réis, with which she intended to pay her owner, Calhelha, for her liberty. The judge accepted Eubrásia's request and appointed a trustee for her, establishing a "depository" (a supervised place of residence) for her and an escrow account for the money.

In January 1882, the slave's trustee, lawyer José Maria Lamaneres, requested that a medical exam be carried out on Eubrásia, alleging that because she was ill and pregnant, her price should be reduced. Calhelha, on the other hand, stressed her "good qualities" and did not accept the amount she offered as deposit. With this impasse began the arbitration over Eubrásia's value.

To carry out the arbitration, each party had to nominate three names, from which the opposing party would choose one. In this case, the master was also able to select the name of another assessor, one who was supposed to be selected by the judge to serve as the third-party arbitrator.

Eubrásia's trustee opposed this nomination, sending a document to the judge on January 2, 1882, which raised suspicions about the assessment of these two arbitrators:

. . . Being friends of the master, being plantation owners who possess large numbers of slaves; and their interest in this is such, that even without having been sworn in, there is already word on the streets that the ward of the supplicant will be assessed at two million *réis*, an absolutely incredible price [i.e., the average price for *two* adult male slaves], but which is said to have been declared by the same arbitrators.

The trustee cited the names of eight people who could attest to what was being said on the streets about Eubrásia. The assessment was temporarily suspended, but after Calhelha complained, the assessment was rescheduled for January 14, 1882. Before the assessment, Eubrásia underwent a medical exam at the request of the trustee. The doctors attested that:

. . . they found nothing indicating any internal or external infirmity, that she was in the seventh month of pregnancy without presenting edemata of the lower limbs or any other symptom that the state of the pregnancy was not regular.

At the assessment hearing, the assessors representing the master and the third party both placed the appropriate value at 1,800,000 réis, while the assessor representing the slave assessed her at 1,000,000 réis. Two days later, Calhelha petitioned the judge for the return of his slave or the presentation of the assessed value. But the slave's lawyer soon petitioned for the cancellation of the arbitration, based on the suspicion that he had raised about the assessors. He argued that "1,000,000 réis is the maximum price that the slave could be worth, and even that is excessive," and he insisted that this would be the maximum price paid.

Since the slave's lawyer petitioned for the cancellation of the arbitration, the judge had to pronounce on this. First, however, he found a series of irregularities in the process, including unpaid fees and the third assessor's lack of explanation for his decision. At the end of the period, he denied the cancellation of the arbitration and ordered that the value of 1,800,000 réis be paid to the master if the slave Eubrásia still wished to purchase her liberty.

The slave's lawyer again questioned this value, saying of Eubrásia, "Along with being old and pregnant, she is not of any utility, being only suited for work in the garden or fields." He contested the master's claims that she was thirty-seven or thirty-eight years old and that she was "suited to all domestic service." As proof, he introduced her registration certificate, dated September 28, 1872. This stated that Eubrásia was black, single, from the fields, and thirty-five years old. If she was thirty-five in 1872, she would be forty-five in 1882.

In his response, Calhelha suggested that the trustee's calculations were wrong. It was strange, he said, "that the Trustee is becoming more and more philanthropic, and less and less proper in the form of the defense . . . so that his ward will be liberated for less than her fair price."

In his final decision, the judge decreed the value of "1,800,000 réis as the price of payment for the liberty of the slave Eubrásia." Yet Eubrásia appealed the decision to the São Paulo Appeals Court and received another trustee, Dr. Manoel Correa Dias. He offered his arguments against the establishment of such a high price for Eubrásia's liberty, noting the necessity to

. . . avoid the bad example of slaves who, having savings, dare to petition for a trustee and depository for the purpose of obliging their masters to liberate them in return for compensation. When an excessive assessment is set, of more than double the savings presented, and being impossible to increase them in the short time frame set, the deposit is returned and the slave restored to the power of the master to receive the rewards for their audacity.

Correa Dias went on to say that "the masters had an interest in raising the price when some slave of theirs had to be assessed to obtain their liberty." Thus they would help other masters in order to "be able to count on their friends and ranchers and demand equal treatment from them under the same circumstances." He concluded by saying that, by proceeding this way, the assessors not only "satisfied the greed of this [master], but also his vanity, offended by his own slave." To prove his arguments, the trustee presented data on the sale of slaves younger than Eubrásia, in better condition to work, who were sold for a much lower price than that arbitrated by the assessors in the process.

The master's lawyers responded by asking the court to affirm Calhelha's position and refuse to authorize Eubrásia the

... extraordinary favors that she invokes, conceded by law to those who plead for their liberty, and this is because the respondent [Calhelha] didn't present the slightest opposition ... [to her freedom], nor sought to interfere in any way with the assessment that the slave ... requested. Since the respondent is the legitimate master and possessor of the slave pursuing freedom, that is, having over her a right recognized by our laws, whose existence in the country he is the first to deplore, but not being responsible for this, he sought from an early date to not interfere with the right that he exercised, aware that there was no incompatibility between this and what was observed to be the compensation of her value, given that this is guaranteed by the very laws protecting liberty, and which she invoked. For all these reasons, he would like to see maintained the assessment that set the compensation for the loss of the services of his slave.

In response, Eubrásia's trustee argued that the "price of slave property" was reduced "to half or less than half of its old value, ... because of the growing abolitionist wave throughout the Empire, because of the repeated killings by slaves of their managers, because of the frequent suicides of the slaves." He added that the decline in prices was an "undeniable fact" that occurred "daily in front of all of us and in the light of day, ... because of the possibility of an unexpected turn in this incandescent issue taken to the bosom of parliament by men of great prestige." In conclusion, he said that Eubrásia, along with being a precarious property "because of the very panic produced by this set of circum-

stances, . . . was simply a black woman, of 45 years of age, with aptitude only for fieldwork."

The Appeals Court ruled on Eubrásia's case on November 10, 1882. The judges decided that the arbitration of 1,800,000 réis was excessive and reduced the value to "1,000,000 réis, a sum they judged reasonable for compensation" of the master. The judges set a deadline of eight days for presentation of the addition to the savings and for Eubrásia's certificate of liberty and condemned the master to pay the costs of the process.

Calhelha's lawyers still tried to block the Appeals Court's judgment with the argument that the judge didn't have the competence to modify the assessment. They also said, "We are not unaware of the privileges that liberation enjoys, and that the law has wisely limited the cases in which it is defended, but there is no necessity to expand them, and nor does the judiciary have the power to do this."

The São Paulo Appeals Court handed down its final decision in favor of Eubrásia, who was emancipated on April 3, 1883.

46

BRAZILIAN CROWN

The Áurea Law: Abolition of Slavery

May 13, 1888

In the late 1880s, the social and political situation changed radically in Brazil. Those regions not connected to coffee production had already lost their slaves. Only the coffee growers of Minas Gerais, São Paulo, and Rio de Janeiro continued to defend slavery and to insist on compensation for masters. However, slaves began to escape en masse, especially in São Paulo. Many imperial soldiers refused orders to recapture the escaped slaves.

The situation was so serious that it threatened the coffee harvest. In this context, even the conservatives from São Paulo began to support immediate abolition in order to obtain reliable workers. The slave

Brazil. *Collecção das Leis do Brasil*, 64 vols. (Rio de Janeiro: Typographia Nacional, 1826–1889), vol. 25, no. 3353. Translated by Mark William Lutes.

establishment in Rio de Janeiro thus became isolated in its opposition to abolition without compensation. Most parliamentarians came around to the view that immediate abolition, with no form of compensation, would be the only way to bring peace to the rural areas.

On May 3, 1888, Princess Isabel signed the Áurea Law, which finally abolished slavery in Brazil. The text of the law is extremely concise. It liberated, without compensation, around 700,000 slaves. With Brazil's abolition, slavery was finally extinct in the Americas, where it had persisted for more than three hundred years. Yet after abolition, Brazil instituted no process for the social inclusion of the freed slaves and their descendants. The freed slaves had no political rights and no access to education, much less to land. They remained like so many other former slaves in the Americas: free, but with few prospects for the future.

Article 1: From the date of enactment of this law slavery is declared extinct.

Article 2: All conflicting legislation is hereby overturned.

5

Epilogue:
The Case of Andrea Quesada,
Cienfuegos, Cuba, 1906–1907

REBECCA SCOTT AND DANIEL NEMSER, WITH THE
ASSISTANCE OF ORLANDO GARCÍA MARTÍNEZ

In the nineteenth century, it was rare for anyone to raise in public the possibility of redress or reparations for those who had been held as slaves. Alleging that an intended manumission had been thwarted, however, opened up a narrow avenue for a legal claim to resources. An unusual case of this kind emerged in the port city of Cienfuegos, in southern Cuba, in 1906. Andrea Quesada, who had been held as a slave on the Santa Rosalía sugar plantation, brought suit against the heirs of her former owner, Manuel Blanco. She asserted that she had been illegally held in bondage for a decade, despite the intent of her prior owner, José Quesada, to free her. She argued that a portion of the Blanco inheritance should now be allocated to her in compensation for the years that she had served Manuel Blanco as a slave.

Because the records of the Santa Rosalía plantation have survived, we know a few things about the woman who brought this case. In 1885, the overseer of the Santa Rosalía plantation had written to the owner,

---

Andrea Quesada's appeal is partially transcribed in a later case, *Martín e Isidora Cabrera de Ávila, contra Cándida Blanco Ramos et al.*, in leg. 459, Secretaría a Cargo de Rafael Roses y Hernández, Civil, Juzgado de Primera Instancia de Cienfuegos, 1927, Archivo Histórico Provincial de Cienfuegos, Cienfuegos, Cuba. Additional materials can be found in the Protocolos Notariales of Verdaguer and Silva Gil in the same archive, and in the Colección Manuscrita Julio Lobo, in the Biblioteca Nacional José Martí, Havana. For a fuller discussion of the case, and detailed citations, see Rebecca J. Scott, *Degrees of Freedom: Louisiana and Cuba after Slavery* (Cambridge, Mass.: Harvard University Press, 2005), pp. 216–23 and 326–28.

Manuel Blanco, to denounce the behavior of the woman he referred to simply as Andrea.

Letter from García, Overseer, to Blanco, Owner, March 15, 1885

I'm writing to tell you that yesterday morning there was a scandal at this plantation produced by Andrea, and then another one like it last night when we were closing up the slave barracks. . . . I ask that you relieve me of my position because I did not come to this plantation to be kicked around by black women, and particularly not of her class, because she's been provoking me to give her a crack on the head but a person has to watch out for himself. . . . She is used to magnetizing everyone who comes to this plantation, [but] I will not be magnetized, not by her or by anyone else. . . . This has been a bad example for the *slaves and the employees* [italics in original]. . . .

A year later, those remaining in bondage on Manuel Blanco's plantation were freed by final abolition, whereupon Andrea Quesada seems to have moved to the port city of Cienfuegos. When Manuel Blanco died intestate twenty years later, his heirs had recourse to the offices of a local notary in Cienfuegos, digging back into the records of the will by which Manuel Blanco had himself inherited the Santa Rosalía estate in 1876. It seems to have been at this moment that Andrea Quesada learned of the existence of an early testament by José Quesada, in which he expressed an intention to confer gracias, *or favors, on his slaves at the time of his death. She wasted no time taking legal steps and filed a power of attorney enabling a local Spanish merchant to represent her.*

Notarial Volumes of Felipe Silva y Gil, May 22, 1906

Señora Andrea Quesada y Acevedo, native and resident of this city, single, dedicated to domestic tasks and sixty-two years old . . . confers full power, as necessary and sufficient unto the requirements of law, upon Señor Domingo Cabrera y Cao,[1] of this city, married, a businessman, and of age, with the following . . . faculties including . . . That he

---

[1] We infer that Domingo Cabrera y Cao and Julián Cabrera y Cao (see below) are either brothers working together or the same person.

may accept, directly or after inventory, the inheritances by will or intestate in which she may have an interest . . . and that he may assist and defend her in litigations, lawsuits, civil and criminal suits. . . . She says thus, being witnesses the señores Braulio Coterón and Eliseo Rangel Jimenez. . . .
[signed Rangel] As witness and signs at the request of the Grantor who does not know how to write.

Word of her initiative appears to have spread quickly among others who had been held as slaves on Santa Rosalía, and they proceeded to draw up similar powers of attorney. Her literate former neighbor Ramón "Ramos" Quesada, who had grown up on the plantation, apparently coordinated these. Within a few months, twenty-seven men and women using the surname Quesada had given powers of attorney either directly or indirectly to Julián Cabrera. Many of them were farmworkers still living in the country. The suit was first argued in the city of Cienfuegos.

Julián Cabrera y Cao, In the Case of *Andreas Quesada* v. *Heirs of Manuel Blanco*, Cienfuegos, April 1907

RESULTING: That Julián Cabrera y Cao . . . established the present lawsuit, which was based on the following FACTS:

First: Don José Quesada y Sada filed a will in the City of Cienfuegos on July 24, 1870, before the Notary Public Don José J. Verdaguer. . . .

Second: Among the goods that he declared as his property figured a Sugar Mill called Santa Rosalía located in the Corral San Antón, District of Cumanayagua, with its equipment, workforce of slaves and animals and other annexes. . . .

Third: In the eleventh clause of the said testament the testator records that it being his will to grant some favors (*gracias*) to his slaves from the workforce of the Santa Rosalía Mill, upon his death a *memoria* [statement] signed by him in which the names and what these favors consisted of would appear, which should be taken as an integral part of the will and consequently should be fulfilled and executed in the terms that were expressed in the same. . . .

[Cabrera y Cao noted that, at the time Quesada's will was drawn up, Blanco appears to have been present as his administrator.]

Fourth: In the twelfth clause Sr. Quesada expresses that in view of having no children nor other necessary heirs and keeping in mind the services that Don Manuel Blanco y Ramos had provided him and who for this reason he considered as if he were his son, instituted and named as his sole and universal heir the previously expressed Don Manuel Blanco y Ramos in order that henceforth he may have, possess and enjoy it with the blessing of God and his own as proof of his affection, to whom he ordered that when his death should occur he take control of all of his goods without need for judicial proceedings and that he should correctly and faithfully fulfill that which the will ordered, as well as that which would appear in the *memoria* in question.

Fifth: On the twenty-first of February of eighteen hundred and seventy six don José Quesada y Sada passed away and from that date forward Don Manuel Blanco y Ramos seized all of the goods, taking possession as was natural of the documents that pertained to the deceased, among those the *memoria* to which the will referred. . . .

Sixth: During the period of time between the death of Don José Quesada y Sada, and that of Don Manuel Blanco y Ramos, Blanco enjoyed all of the goods that belonged to Quesada, without bothering to fulfill the demands of the *memoria* that constituted, as the eleventh clause states, an "integral part" of the will and should have been fulfilled and executed in the terms in which it was expressed.

Seventh: As a consequence of the failure to comply with that called for by the testator Sr. Quesada in the aforementioned document that constituted an integral part of his last will, the slaves of the Santa Rosalía Sugar Mill remained slaves until their liberty was decreed by the Spanish parliament, at which time don Manuel Blanco y Ramos was held in high esteem in the city of Cienfuegos and enjoyed the abundant goods that were left to him upon the death of Sr. Quesada.

Eighth: Among these slaves figured my client Andrea Quesada, who has learned that she is one of the beneficiaries named in the *memoria* that Don José Quesada y Sada left and in spite of this her fate remained the same as that of her fellow workers, she did not receive the favor that her owner, of his free and spontaneous will, bestowed upon her. . . .

Ninth: Because Don Manuel Blanco y Ramos failed to comply with the will of the testator Sr. Quesada, my client, having now received news that the defendants . . . had declared themselves his heirs, filed suit *en conciliación* [in settlement] to oblige them to present the aforementioned *memoria* or, in its place, the documents that would prove the fulfillment of that which Don José Quesada y Sada arranged; and as the action was scheduled for the eighteenth of the month at one in the afternoon, but those named did not appear before the court, this effort at conciliation is deemed to have been attempted. . . . The plaintiff's representative, after asserting the principles of law that he believed applicable, concluded by requesting that the demand be forwarded and by making a claim for declaratory judgment . . . against the defendants, and requesting that the case be resolved in the following terms:

First: To order the heirs of the intestate Don Manuel Blanco y Ramos to present the *memoria* signed by Don José Quesada y Sada in which he disposed of various bequests in favor of the slaves that made up the workforce of the Santa Rosalía Sugar Mill, among them figuring the plaintiff Andrea Quesada. . . .

Second: To order that if they do not present the *memoria* that has so many times been named, nor other documents that accredit and prove the fulfillment of what it ordered, the heirs of Don Manuel Blanco y Ramos must abstain from occupying or possessing the goods left upon his death, because not being heirs themselves of Don José Quesada y Sada, but rather of Don Manuel Blanco y Ramos, as long as Quesada's solemnly expressed will is not fulfilled, it remains unknown which goods belong to Don Manuel Blanco y Ramos and therefore those which the defendants can inherit.

Third: To declare that, as a consequence, the effects of the *memoria* written by D. José Quesada y Sada in his testament at the moment of his death be made retroactive, such that his goods may be distributed among those to whom they rightfully belong, as was established by the testator and be passed to those who can establish their right to them. . . .

Fourth: . . . I ask that it be decreed that the administration of the goods that constitute D. Manuel Blanco y Ramos's wealth be turned over to a person designated by the court, in order to prevent those who declared themselves heirs of D. Manuel Blanco y Ramos from disposing of the goods that are attached to the responsibilities that the testator Quesada imposed, which would make the rights of his client and others who find themselves in this situation impossible to claim.

The attorney for the defense, Emilio Menéndez, responded.

Emilio Menéndez, In the Case of *Andreas Quesada v. Heirs of Manuel Blanco*, Cienfuegos, April 1907

. . .

Third: My clients have no knowledge of the *memoria*'s having been found upon the death of Don José Quesada. . . .

Fourth: Quesada passed away on the twenty-first of February of eighteen seventy-six and this lawsuit seeking the fulfillment of his will has been filed against the surviving heirs of the heir Manuel Blanco y Ramos after thirty years have passed.

Fifth: For this attack against the pockets of my clients to not even prosper, but simply have any cover to its crude grasping, the plaintiff would have to prove, and not merely assume as she does, the following propositions:

First: The existence of the testamentary *memoria*; that is to say, that Quesada carried out the intention announced in his testament of drafting said *memoria* and that Manuel Blanco took possession of it, upon the death of the testator.

Second: That the plaintiff is one of the beneficiaries to which said *memoria* makes reference.

Third: That the favor or bequest that the testator made to the plaintiff was that of granting her liberty. . . .

[Menéndez concluded by denying the plaintiff's charges. He called for her case to be dismissed on the grounds of her lack of cause of action, her lack of standing to bring suit (she did not prove that she was an heir) and prescripción, *a concept similar to a statute of limitations.]*

Julián Cabrera y Cao, Representing Andrea Quesada, Reply, 1907

. . .

Second: . . . The plaintiff learned the news about being one of the beneficiaries (*agraciadas*) from the 1870 testament, whose existence she learned of only on the date on which she requested a copy of it and it was ordered to be given to her by the Judge of First Instance of this City, a copy of which accompanied the lawsuit. By this document, she learned that all of the slaves of the Santa Rosalía Sugar Mill had been named beneficiaries by her owner D. José Quesada y Sada and as she had been a slave of the cited Sugar Mill, it is clear that she is one of the heirs of the testator. . . .

Fifth: . . . It is not correct that the eleventh clause of the will of Sr. José Quesada y Sada says what the representative of the defendants attributes to it. This clause says textually the following: "I declare that it being my will to grant some favors to my slaves of the workforce of the Santa Rosalía Sugar Mill upon my death a *memoria* signed by me will be found in which the names and what said favors consist of will appear, which *memoria* I wish to be taken as an integral part of this testament and that consequently it should be fulfilled and executed in the terms that are expressed here." Therefore, there is no limitation about the favors being granted only to several of the slaves of the Santa Rosalía Sugar Mill. All of the slaves, absolutely all, turned out to be beneficiaries according to the testament. The quantity of the gift or bequest to each one, was what the *memoria* determined, according to the clear and explicit words of the testator. It is clear what end the other side is pursuing by the alteration that they are making: That of demanding that Andrea Quesada had to prove that she was a beneficiary. But the opposing representation thinks one thing, and another, very different thing appears in the testamentary clause that was left behind. Andrea Quesada, slave of the Santa Rosalía Sugar Mill, is heir of D. José Quesada y Sada by his solemnly expressed will, without need of another demonstration than that which she has presented from the testament and the document that justifies that she was a slave of Santa Rosalía.

Sixth: ... The affirmation that ... the defendants have no knowledge of the fact that upon the death of D. José Quesada y Sada the *memoria* to which the testament alludes would be found, is nothing but an evasion to dodge the difficulties and the predicament in which the defendants find themselves. It is not enough to say that they did not know of the *memoria*'s having been found, because this says nothing. The lawsuit that Andrea Quesada is exercising is born in the testament. It says that the *memoria* written by the testator had to be fulfilled by the executor, so the burden of proof is on him and his successors in interest to demonstrate that it was fulfilled, since there exists no motive to doubt the existence of the *memoria*. ...

Seventh: ... It is curious that it is being affirmed that ... because thirty years have passed since the death of the testator, Andrea Quesada is unable to demand that they fulfill the will of Sr. Quesada, when for her, it has only been just barely one year since she found out that the testament of D. José Quesada y Sada existed and that in it gifts, bequests and favors are discussed, in favor of the slaves of the Santa Rosalía Sugar Mill. It is as if the defendants had taken good care to avoid saying a word about this, in order to prevent what, in the end, was bound to happen, that the poor slaves would learn about the existence of the testamentary provision, and *that someone would take up the cause of justice, right, and humanity* [italics in original]. . . .

Judge Antonio J. Varona, Ruling, April 12, 1907

CONSIDERING: . . . The proof of obligations always rests with the plaintiff, since she affirms the truth of the facts that support her suit; for which reasons it is unarguable that the plaintiff should have justified the existence and authenticity of the testamentary *memoria* out of which comes the right that she exercises, and [established] what said *memoria* consists of, and what favor by the same should come to her; because, although those are the principal points from which her rights could arise, we should not forget that the validity and the efficacy of testamentary *memorias* depend, not only on the special mention given in the testament, but also on establishing the consistency of any such memoria with its mention in the testament. . . .

CONSIDERING: That not having established these points, the current suit lacks basis and, therefore, the plaintiff lacks a cause of action, because one cannot accept logically that because the defendants claim to have no knowledge of the finding of the *memoria* upon the death of Sr. Quesada, this somehow proves the *memoria*'s existence, even though the testator expressly declared that upon his death such a *memoria* that had to be taken as integral part of his testament would be found. The testator's declaration of intention does not mean that he carried it out. . . .

CONSIDERING: That even though in the public document on page sixteen, filed by the plaintiff in her suit, it is justified that the creole black woman Andrea of the personnel of the Santa Rosalía Sugar Mill in the year eighteen hundred seventy one was a slave of Don José Quesada, this fact alone does not demonstrate her legal standing, denied by the defendants . . . because for this the existence of the testamentary *memoria* would have to be proven. . . . Thus it is proper to declare admissible the defendants' objection on the grounds of lack of legal standing.

CONSIDERING: That even if it were the case that the plaintiff in this instance had a cause of action to bring the present suit, such action had expired after the passage of thirty years from the death of the testator Sr. Quesada, because the time limit for requesting a favor or bequest to which one claims a right should be calculated from the date of his death.

I FIND: That I should and do declare inadmissible the present lawsuit established by Julián Cabrera y Cao in the name of Andrea Quesada y Acevedo against the defendants ... whom I absolve of guilt; and likewise I should and do declare admissible the affirmative defenses (*excepciones*) of lack of cause of action and lack of legal standing of the plaintiff, and expiration by virtue of the statute of limitations as alleged by the defendants; without special liability for court costs and, therefore, without declaring any of the litigants reckless or in bad faith.... By this my ruling I thus declare, order and sign...Antonio J. Varona... Cienfuegos April twelfth of nineteen hundred and seven....

Andrea Quesada and her allies, however, were not deterred. By this point, the case seems to have taken on a certain momentum in the community, and there were at least twenty-five other former slaves from Santa Rosalía waiting to see whether the Blanco inheritance could be tapped into. Andrea Quesada's senior legal counsel, Benito A. Besada, was a prominent liberal politician in the provincial capital of Santa Clara and may have had his own reasons for remaining involved with the case. Along with a new legal representative, Emilio G. Coya, they appealed the case to the Superior Court (Audiencia) of the Province of Santa Clara, which issued the following decision.

Franco. F. de la Torre, Alberto Ortiz, Wenceslao Gálvez, The Magistrate Alberto F. Diago, and Raúl Trelles, Superior Court Decision, May 12, 1908

CONSIDERING: .... The affirmative defense of lack of legal standing on the part of the plaintiff, which must consist necessarily of the plaintiff's lacking the necessary attributes to appear before the court or not demonstrating eligibility to make the claim in question ... should not be confused with the lack of cause of action, which affects the efficacy of the rights that are being claimed; as a result in the present case, in which the plaintiff exercises her own rights and is not incapacitated from appearing before the court, the alleged affirmative defense of lack of legal standing is inadmissible, since the fact of her having been or not a slave of the testator either gives her or does not give her the right to claim the bequest announced in the testament, according to the terms that were to be stipulated in the testamentary *memoria*; without affecting in any way her legal standing. ....

WE FIND: That we should and do declare inadmissible the affirmative defense of lack of legal standing on the part of the plaintiff and admissible the affirmative defenses of lack of cause of action and pre-scription, and as a consequence we must declare and we declare inad-missible the lawsuit, absolving the defendants of the charges. . . . We confirm the appealed sentence in that which is consistent and for that which is not we revoke it. . . . Thusly, by this our sentence we pro-nounce, order and sign it. Raúl Trelles. Franco. F. de la Torre. Alberto Ortiz. Wenceslao Gálvez. The Magistrate Alberto F. Diago voted in his chambers and was unable to sign. Raúl Trelles.

Having established the bare minimum—that she, a former slave, was possessed of judicial personality appropriate to the suit at hand—Andrea Quesada and her allies appealed the case to the Supreme Court of Cuba. As an elderly resident of a community near Santa Rosalía recalls it, on the way to Havana for the final stage of the suit, Ramos Quesada, Andrea's neighbor and ally, stopped to chat with a neighbor. The neigh-bor told him that it was useless to try to defeat in court a family as pow-erful as that of Manuel Blanco. Ramos Quesada replied, "Even without money, we are going to put up a fight. At least we will make things clear."[2] The Supreme Court, however, gave them short shrift. On Decem-ber 8, 1908, their appeal was rejected and the case closed.

Was the law, in this instance, empowering or merely entangling? On one reading, Andrea Quesada, Ramos Quesada, and the others had wasted time and resources fighting against a family that had the power to hold on to property and to ignore inconvenient documents. On an-other reading, however, the public assertion of standing by a group of for-mer slaves, and the political alliances that Andrea and Ramos Quesada wove with a white politician from Santa Clara, are emblematic of an important set of claims-making strategies available in post-emancipation Cuba. The Cuban political system, with its guarantee of universal man-hood suffrage, gave electoral weight to the men in the group and reinforced a public culture in which an assertive woman like Andrea Quesada could exercise judicial agency.

Formally, the island was under a second military occupation by the United States that would last until 1909. But in the world of the courts, this was a matter to be resolved among Cubans. Furthermore, in the countryside around Santa Rosalía, the deeper morality of the question, and the public perception of each of the protagonists, would be estab-lished by those who knew the principals. Ninety years later, two re-

---

[2]Interview by Rebecca Scott, Orlando García Martínez, and Michael Zeuske with Marcelino Iznaga Suárez Román, Cienfuegos, 2002.

searchers utterly unaware of the case interviewed a man who had worked on Santa Rosalía, who was himself probably equally unaware of the lost lawsuit. But he had heard a rumor about the will of José Quesada. The old man, he said, had intended to leave the entire plantation to his slaves, but Manuel Blanco had cheated them out of it.[3]

We will never know what, precisely, the ailing José Quesada intended on the day that Manuel Blanco stood at his side as he filed a set of documents with the notary. But if current residents of Cienfuegos hold him to have had generous intentions, and the former slaves to have been cheated out of their rights, Andrea Quesada's very public legal action may be partly responsible. In popular memory, the case took on a second life, transforming itself from a limited demand for recompense into a broad claim to the land itself.

---

[3]Interview by Rebecca Scott and Orlando García Martínez with Sebastián Asla Cires, Rancho Luna, Cuba, 1997.

A Chronology of the History of Slavery, Antislavery, and Emancipation (1265–1888)

1265   Castilian king Alfonso X issues *Las Siete Partidas*, a comprehensive legal code that forms the basis for all future Spanish slave legislation.

1340s   The Portuguese begin direct slave raids and trading in the Canary Islands.

1441   Explorers return to Portugal from Senegal with the first African slaves imported via the Atlantic, rather than the Saharan, trade.

1502   The first enslaved Africans arrive in Spanish America.

1520   The Spanish crown grants the first slave-trade charters.

1538   The first ship of African slaves arrives in Brazil.

1564   England enters the slave trade.

1590s   Cuban records frequently mention the practice of *coartación*, or gradual self-purchase. The practice is likely much older and is consistent with both Islamic and medieval Spanish slave law.

1603   King Philip II issues the *Ordenações Filipinas*, which regulate slavery throughout the Portuguese empire.

1619   Enslaved Africans arrive in the English settlement of Jamestown, Virginia.

1625   England settles Barbados.

1635   France establishes the colonies of Guadeloupe and Martinique in the Caribbean, mainly to produce tobacco.

1654   The Portuguese expel the Dutch and the Jews from Brazil; the refugees bring technological expertise and slaves to French, Dutch, and English settlements in the Caribbean.

1664   The French government issues its first license for the African slave trade to the Compagnie des Indes Occidentales (West India Company).

1685   The French crown issues the *Code Noir*, the first comprehensive slave law code in the Americas.

178

1688   Early Quakers protest the slave trade in Pennsylvania.

1695   Palmares, the largest maroon community in Brazil, is destroyed after one hundred years of war.

1713   The British win the Spanish *asiento* (exclusive transatlantic slave-trading contract) from France.

1716   Royal edict permits slaveholders to bring their slaves to France, but the penalty for nonregistration is the slaves' freedom.

1734   Portuguese royal law first mentions liberty as a reward for good services provided by slaves.

1739   Jamaica's First Maroon War (1700–1739) concludes with a treaty between the British and the maroons.

1755   The *Lei da Liberdade* (Freedom Law) recognizes the full liberty of indigenous peoples within the Portuguese empire.

1761   Royal proclamation frees all slaves who arrive in Portugal.

1772   Judge Mansfield rules in London that the slave James Somerset cannot be compelled by his master to return to the colonies. This decision is widely interpreted as abolishing slavery in England.

1776   The thirteen colonies of the United States declare independence from England.

1777   The republic of Vermont declares independence from England. Its constitution outlaws slavery and allows all adult males to vote.

1777   Royal legislation, the *Police des Noirs*, prohibits the entry of all "blacks, mulattoes and other people of color" into France.

1778   In *Knight v. Wedderburn*, the Scottish high court rules that enslavement is incompatible with national law.

1780   Pennsylvania passes a gradual emancipation law, freeing children born to slave parents, though they owe service until the age of twenty-eight.

1783   On a slave-trading run from Africa to Jamaica in 1781, the captain of the ship *Zong* threw 131 sick Africans overboard. Upon the captain's return to England, his case is heard as an insurance dispute, not a murder trial, causing public outrage.

1787   The U.S. Constitution permits slavery, counting each slave as three-fifths of a person for taxation and representation purposes; it forbids the banning of the slave trade before 1808.

1788   Abolitionists circulate public petitions, signed by thousands of citizens, urging the end of the slave trade in England.

1789   Black abolitionist Olaudah Equiano publishes his book, *The Interesting Narrative of the Life of Olaudah Equiano, or Gustavus Vassa, the African*, in England.

1789 The French National Assembly issues the Declaration of Rights of Man and Citizen; the French Revolution begins.

1790 William Wilberforce presents the first bill to abolish the slave trade to the British House of Commons, but it does not pass.

1791 A slave revolt breaks out on the northern plains of the French Caribbean colony of Saint-Domingue; the Haitian Revolution begins.

1793 French republican commissioners abolish slavery in Saint-Domingue.

1794 The French revolutionary government abolishes slavery throughout the French empire.

1802 Napoléon declares the restoration of slavery in the French empire. His armies attempt to impose this by force in Saint-Domingue but are repelled by insurgents. The people of Guadeloupe resist the return of slavery but are defeated in battle.

1802 The French army entraps Toussaint-Louverture, a former slave, a brilliant general, and at the time of his capture the governor-for-life of Saint-Domingue. They transport him to a prison in France, where he dies in 1803.

1804 Jean-Jacques Dessalines declares Haiti independent.

1805 Haiti's first constitution abolishes slavery and denies whites the right to own property.

1807 The U.S. Congress and the British Parliament independently ban the transatlantic slave trade. The U.S. ban takes effect on January 1, 1808.

1808 The Portuguese royal family, running from Napoléon's army, arrives in Brazil. Brazilian ports open to friendly nations, especially England.

1811 Argentina and Venezuela declare independence from Spain.

1813 Argentina passes a gradual emancipation law.

1815 At the Congress of Vienna, concluding the Napoleonic Wars, Britain pressures Spain, Portugal, France, and the Netherlands to agree to abolish the slave trade. However, Spain and Portugal are permitted a few years of continued slaving to replenish labor supplies, and the French ban is not enforced.

1816 A major slave rebellion occurs in the British colony of Barbados.

1817 Spain signs a treaty with England, agreeing to end the Spanish slave trade north of the equator immediately and south of the equator in 1820.

1818 Chile declares independence from Spain.

1819   Colombia declares independence from Spain.

1821   The region that today comprises Ecuador, Colombia, and Venezuela adopts a gradual emancipation plan.

1821   Mexico declares independence from Spain.

1822   Brazil declares independence from Portugal.

1822   Ecuador declares independence from Spain.

1823   Chile abolishes slavery.

1823   British forces brutally suppress a slave revolt in the British South American colony of Demerara.

1824   Peru declares independence from Spain.

1824   The first constitution of independent Brazil affirms civil rights, though not political rights, for former slaves.

1825   Bolivia declares independence from Spain.

1825   France recognizes independent Haiti but requires that the new nation of former slaves pay 100 million livres in reparations for the loss of slaveholders' property.

1826   Brazil and Britain sign a treaty prohibiting the entry of African slaves into Brazil, but its effectiveness is undermined by continued smuggling.

1829   Mexico abolishes slavery.

1831   Brazil issues the "law for the English to see," ostensibly banishing the slave trade, but it remains unenforced.

1831   British forces brutally suppress a major slave revolt in Jamaica.

1831   French forces suppress a slave revolt in Martinique.

1831   Nat Turner leads a slave revolt in Virginia.

1831   Bolivia abolishes slavery.

1833   Britain abolishes slavery throughout the British Empire by an apprenticeship system, initially requiring that slaves provide six more years of labor, later reduced to four.

1835   Slaves in Bahia, Brazil, rise up in the largest urban slave revolt in the Americas.

1838   Slaves are emancipated in the British territories. Colonial assemblies pass laws against vagrancy and squatting to support the planters' interests. Former slaves are not permitted to vote.

1839   African slaves aboard the Spanish ship *Amistad* revolt near Cuba. The U.S. Supreme Court rules in favor of their freedom in 1841.

1841   Slaves revolt in Havana, Cuba.

1842   Cuba issues a new, restrictive slave code.

1845   The British Parliament passes the Aberdeen Act, legalizing the seizure of Brazilian ships involved in the slave trade.

1848   As part of a liberal revolution in France, slavery is permanently abolished throughout the French Empire.

1850   Brazil bans the Atlantic slave trade without revoking the 1831 law.

1854   Slavery is abolished in Peru.

1857   The U.S. Supreme Court rules that Dred Scott has no legal personality as a black man and cannot sue for his freedom, regardless of whether he has set foot on free territory.

1865   The Thirteenth Amendment to the U.S. Constitution abolishes slavery.

1868   The Fourteenth Amendment to the U.S. Constitution guarantees equal rights to all citizens.

1868   The Fifteenth Amendment to the U.S. Constitution forbids discrimination on the basis of race, color, or previous enslavement.

1871   Brazil passes the gradualist Free Womb Law, granting freedom to slaves born after this date, upon the age of eight or twenty-one (at the master's discretion).

1886   Cuba abolishes slavery.

1888   Brazil abolishes slavery.

Questions for Consideration

1. Define *slavery;* define *freedom.* Are these definitions universal, or do they vary by time, place, and circumstance?

2. What facts, laws, or situations did you find surprising in these documents? How did they challenge your understanding of slavery or freedom?

3. What are some different means by which individual slaves might have gained their freedom? How did these different paths to freedom affect the actions of slaves, masters, free people of color, and government officials?

4. What difference did gender make for slaves or free people of color? How did men and women experience slavery, manumission, and citizenship differently?

5. When slaves filed lawsuits for freedom, what did they risk, and what specifically did they stand to gain? How did participation in a lawsuit change both the litigant and his or her community?

6. As laws created avenues for slaves to become free—whether individually or as an entire class—how did racial language in the law work to redefine or undermine that freedom? Were racial categories and privileges identical in all societies?

7. Contrast manumission (the freeing of an individual slave) with general emancipation (the abolition of slavery throughout a nation-state). Did freedom mean the same thing in each situation?

8. Do you see important changes or trends over time? For example, were the relationships between masters, slaves, and free people of color defined differently in eighteenth-century legal documents than in nineteenth-century documents? How did the rhetoric and vocabulary change? How do you explain such changes?

9. How were the legal arguments about slavery and freedom related to emerging notions of citizenship and nationality?

10. What do you see as interesting similarities between slave law and society in the French, British, Spanish, and Portuguese empires and their subsequent independent American nation-states? What do you see as significant differences? How do you explain these differences?

11. How do the documents suggest that ideas about freedom in one society might have influenced other societies?

12. Who were these texts—documents and illustrations—created for? Who would have had access to them, and who would not? How might various audiences have interpreted each document differently?

Selected Bibliography

Thousands of books and articles have been written on the history of slavery in the Americas. These are just a sampling of works related primarily to slave law to give students a head start on further research in the area. They are a mix of relatively recent works and classics in the field.

INTERNET RESOURCES

Many vivid illustrations by Guamán Poma of the Spanish conquest of Peru can be found at the Web site of the Danish Royal Library: http://www.kb .dk/elib/mss/poma/index-en.htm.

University of Virginia scholars Jerome S. Handler and Michael L. Tuite Jr. have compiled a searchable database of images of slavery, "The Atlantic Slave Trade and Slave Life in the Americas: A Visual Record": http://hitchcock.itc.virginia.edu/Slavery/.

Sue Peabody maintains a guide to many Web sites pertaining to the history of slavery: http://www.vancouver.wsu.edu/fac/peabody/slave.htm.

GENERAL

Blackburn, Robin. *The Overthrow of Colonial Slavery, 1776–1848*. London: Verso, 1988.

Davis, David Brion. *Inhuman Bondage: The Rise and Fall of Slavery in the New World*. New York: Oxford University Press, 2006.

———. *The Problem of Slavery in the Age of Revolution, 1770–1823*. Ithaca, N.Y.: Cornell University Press, 1975.

Drescher, Seymour, and Stanley L. Engerman, eds. *A Historical Guide to World Slavery*. New York: Oxford University Press, 1998.

Handler, Jerome, and Annis Steiner. "Identifying Pictorial Images of Atlantic Slavery: Three Case Studies." *Slavery and Abolition*, 27 (2006): 56–62.

Heuman, Gad, and James Walvin, eds. *The Slavery Reader*. London: Routledge, 2003.

Klein, Herbert S. *African Slavery in Latin America and the Caribbean*. New York: Oxford University Press, 1986.

Tannenbaum, Frank. *Slave and Citizen.* Boston: Beacon Press, 1992. First published 1946.

Watson, Alan. *Slave Law in the Americas.* Athens: University of Georgia Press, 1989.

FRENCH ATLANTIC

Dubois, Laurent. *A Colony of Citizens: Revolution and Slave Emancipation in the French Caribbean, 1787–1804.* Omohundro Institute of Early American History and Culture. Chapel Hill: University of North Carolina Press, 2004.

———, and John D. Garrigus. *Slave Revolution in the Caribbean, 1789–1804: A Brief History with Documents.* Boston: Bedford/St. Martin's, 2006.

Fick, Carolyn E. *The Making of Haiti: The Saint Domingue Revolution from Below.* Knoxville: University of Tennessee Press, 1990.

Garrigus, John D. *Before Haiti: Race and Citizenship in French Saint-Domingue.* New York: Palgrave Macmillan, 2006.

Geggus, David P., ed. *The Impact of the Haitian Revolution in the Atlantic World.* Charleston: University of South Carolina Press, 2001.

Klein, Martin A. *Slavery and Colonial Rule in French West Africa.* Cambridge: Cambridge University Press, 1998.

Palmer, Vernon V. "The Origins and Authors of the *Code Noir.*" In *An Uncommon Experience: Law and Judicial Institutions in Louisiana, 1803–2003,* edited by Judith Schaeffer and Warren M. Billings, 331–59. Lafayette: Center for Louisiana Studies, University of Southwestern Louisiana, 1997.

Peabody, Sue. *"There Are No Slaves in France": The Political Culture of Race and Slavery in the Ancien Régime.* New York: Oxford University Press, 1996.

Rogers, Dominique. "Les libres de couleur dans les capitales de Saint-Domingue: Fortune, mentalités et integration à la fin de l'Ancien Régime (1776–1789)." PhD diss., Université de Bordeaux-III, 1999.

———. "Les libres de couleur et la société domingoise à la fin de l'Ancien Régime: Au-delà des représentations," *Catalogue d'exposition Des constitutions à la Description de Saint-Domingue, la colonie française vue par Moreau de Saint-Méry.* Fort-de-France, Martinique: Archives Départementales de la Martinique, 2004.

Savage, John. "Between Colonial Fact and French Law: Slave Poisoning and the Provostial Court in Restoration Era Martinique." *French Historical Studies,* 29, no. 4 (2006): 620–60.

———. "'Black Magic' and White Terror: Slave Poisoning and Colonial Society in Early Nineteenth-Century Martinique." *Journal of Social History,* 40, no. 3 (Spring 2007).

————. "Unwanted Slaves: The Punishment of Transportation and the Making of Legal Subjects in Early 19th Century Martinique." In "Citizenship Struggles in North America and the Caribbean," edited by H. Amani Whitfield and Bridgett Williams-Searle, special issue, *Citizenship Studies*, 10, no. 1 (2006): 35–53.

Sheller, Mimi. *Democracy after Slavery: Black Publics and Peasant Radicalism in Haiti and Jamaica.* Gainesville: University Press of Florida, 2000.

Stein, Robert Louis. *The French Slave Trade in the Eighteenth Century: An Old Regime Business.* Madison: University of Wisconsin Press, 1979.

Vaughan, Megan. *Creating the Creole Island: Slavery in Eighteenth-Century Mauritius.* Durham, N.C.: Duke University Press, 2005.

BRITISH ATLANTIC AND THE UNITED STATES

Bauer, Carol Phillips. "Law, Slavery and Somersett's Case in Eighteenth Century England: A Study of the Legal Status of Freedom." PhD diss., New York University, 1973.

Berlin, Ira. *Many Thousands Gone: The First Two Centuries of Slavery in North America.* Cambridge, Mass.: Belknap Press of Harvard University Press, 1998.

Bilby, Kenneth. "Swearing by the Past, Swearing to the Future: Sacred Oaths, Alliances and Treaties among the Guianese and Jamaican Maroons." *Ethnohistory*, 44, no. 4 (Fall 1997): 655–89.

Brown, Christopher Leslie. *Moral Capital: Foundations of British Abolitionism.* Omohundro Institute of Early American History and Culture. Chapel Hill: University of North Carolina Press, 2006.

Campbell, Mavis C. *The Maroons of Jamaica, 1655–1796: A History of Resistance, Collaboration and Betrayal.* Trenton, N.J.: Africa World Press, 1990.

Catterall, Helen. *Judicial Cases concerning American Slavery and the Negro.* 5 vols. Buffalo: W. S. Hein, 1998. First published 1932.

Cohen, William. "Negro Involuntary Servitude in the South, 1865–1940: A Preliminary Analysis." *Journal of Southern History*, 42, no. 1 (1976): 31–60.

Equiano, Olaudah. *The Interesting Narrative of the Life of Olaudah Equiano: Written by Himself, with Related Documents.* 2nd ed. Edited by Robert J. Allison. Boston: Bedford/St. Martin's, 2007.

Finkelman, Paul. *Defending Slavery: Proslavery Thought in the Old South; A Brief History with Documents.* Boston: Bedford/St. Martin's, 2003.

————. *Dred Scott v. Sandford: A Brief History with Documents.* Boston: Bedford/St. Martin's, 1997.

————. *The Law of Freedom and Bondage: A Casebook.* New York: Oceana, 1986.

———. "'Let Justice Be Done, Though the Heavens May Fall': The Law of Freedom." *Chicago-Kent Law Review* (1994): 325–68.

———. *Slavery in the Courtroom.* Union, N.J.: Lawbook Exchange, 1998.

Higginbotham, A. Leon, Jr. *In the Matter of Color: Race and the American Legal Process: The Colonial Period.* New York: Oxford University Press, 1978.

Morris, Thomas D. *Southern Slavery and the Law, 1619–1860.* Chapel Hill: University of North Carolina Press, 1996.

Nash, Gary B. *Forging Freedom: The Formation of Philadelphia's Black Community, 1720–1840.* Cambridge, Mass.: Harvard University Press, 1988.

———, and Jean R. Soderlund. *Freedom by Degrees: Emancipation in Pennsylvania and Its Aftermath.* New York: Oxford University Press, 1991.

Oakes, James. "'The Compromising Expedient': Justifying a Proslavery Constitution." *Cardozo Law Review,* 17 (1996): 2023–56. *Academic Universe, Lexis/Nexis* (accessed February 20, 2004).

Pease, Jane H., and William H. Pease. *The Fugitive Slave Law and Anthony Burns: A Problem in Law Enforcement.* Edited by Harold M. Hyman. America's Alternative Series. Philadelphia: J. B. Lippincott, 1975.

Price, Richard. *Maroon Societies: Rebel Slave Communities in the Americas.* Baltimore: Johns Hopkins University Press, 1973. Reprint, 1987.

Schaeffer, Judith Kelleher. *Becoming Free, Remaining Free: Manumission and Enslavement in New Orleans, 1846–1862.* Baton Rouge: Louisiana State University Press, 2003.

———. *Slavery, the Civil Law, and the Supreme Court of Louisiana.* Baton Rouge: Louisiana State University Press, 1994.

Vorenberg, Michael. *Final Freedom: The Civil War, the Abolition of Slavery, and the Thirteenth Amendment.* Cambridge: Cambridge University Press, 2001.

White, Ashli. "'A Flood of Impure Lava': Saint Dominguan Refugees in the United States, 1791–1820." PhD diss., Columbia University, 2003.

Wiecek, William. *The Sources of Antislavery Constitutionalism in America, 1760–1848.* London: Cornell University Press, 1977.

Zilversmit, Arthur. *The First Emancipation: The Abolition of Slavery in the North.* Chicago: University of Chicago Press, 1967.

SPANISH AMERICA

Aguirre, Carlos. "Working the System: Black Slaves and the Courts in Lima, Peru, 1821–1854." In *Crossing Boundaries: Comparative History of Black People in Diaspora,* 202–22, edited by Darlene C. Hine and Jacqueline McLeod. Bloomington: Indiana University Press, 1999.

Blanchard, Peter. *Slavery and Abolition in Early Republican Peru:* Latin American Silhouettes. Wilmington, Del.: SR Books, 1992.

Corbitt, Arthur. *Spain and Abolition of Slavery in Cuba, 1817–1886.* Austin: University of Texas Press, 1967.

Ferrer, Ada. *Insurgent Cuba: Race, Nation and Revolution, 1868–1898.* Chapel Hill: University of North Carolina Press, 1999.

Hunefeldt, Christine. *Paying the Price of Freedom: Family and Labor among Lima's Slaves, 1800–1854.* Berkeley and Los Angeles: University of California Press, 1994.

Knight, Franklin. *Slave Society in Cuba during the Nineteenth Century.* Madison: University of Wisconsin Press, 1970.

Lucena, Manuel. *Leyes para esclavos: El ordenamiento jurídico sobre la condición, tratamiento, defensa y represión de los esclavos en las colónias de la América española.* Madrid: Fundación Histórica Tavera, 2000.

Ortiz, F. *Los negros esclavos.* Havana: Editorial de Ciencias Sociales, 1996.

Scott, Rebecca J. *Slave Emancipation in Cuba: The Transition to Free Labor, 1860–1899.* Princeton, N.J.: Princeton University Press, 1985.

Torres-Cuevas, Eduardo, and Eusebio Reyes. *Esclavitud y sociedad: Notas y documentos para la historia de la esclavitud negra en Cuba.* Havana: Editorial de Ciencias Sociales, 1986.

BRAZIL

Chalhoub, Sidney. "Slaves, Freedmen and the Politics of Freedom in Brazil: The Experience of Blacks in the City of Rio." *Slavery and Abolition,* 10 (December 1989): 64–84.

———. *Visões da liberdade: Uma história das últimas décadas da escravidão na Corte.* São Paulo: Companhia das Letras, 1990.

Conrad, Robert Edgar. *Brazilian Slavery: An Annotated Research Bibliography.* Boston: G. K. Hall, 1977.

———. *Children of God's Fire: A Documentary History of Black Slavery in Brazil.* University Park: Pennsylvania State University Press, 1994.

———. *The Destruction of Brazilian Slavery, 1850–1888.* 2nd ed. Malabar, Fla.: Krieger, 1993.

Costa, Emília Viotti da. *The Brazilian Empire: Myths and Histories.* Chicago: University of Chicago Press, 1985.

Degler, Carl N. *Neither Black nor White: Slavery and Race Relations in Brazil and the United States.* Madison: University of Wisconsin Press, 1986.

Eisenberg, Peter L. *The Sugar Industry in Pernambuco: Modernization without Change, 1840–1910.* Berkeley and Los Angeles: University of California Press, 1974.

Grinberg, Keila. *Liberata: A lei da ambigüidade.* Rio de Janeiro: Relume Dumará, 1994.

Karasch, Mary C. *Slave Life in Rio de Janeiro, 1808–1850.* Princeton, N.J.: Princeton University Press, 1987.

Lara, Silvia. *Legislação sobre escravos africanos na América Portuguesa.* Madrid: Fundación Histórica Tavera, 2000.

Mattos, Hebe. *Das cores do silêncio: Os significados da liberdade no sudeste escravista—Brasil séc. XIX.* Rio de Janeiro: Nova Fronteira, 1998.

Paiva, Eduardo França. *Escravos e libertos em minas gerais: Estratégias de resistência através de testamentos.* São Paulo: Annablume, 1995.

Reis, João José. *Slave Rebellion in Brazil: The Muslim Uprising of 1835 in Bahia.* Baltimore: Johns Hopkins University Press, 1993.

Russell-Wood, A. J. R. *The Black Man in Slavery and Freedom in Colonial Brazil.* New York: St. Martin's Press, 1982.

Schwartz, Stuart B. *Slaves, Peasants, and Rebels: Reconsidering Brazilian Slavery.* Urbana: University of Illinois Press, 1992.

———. *Sugar Plantations in the Formation of Brazilian Society: Bahia, 1550–1835.* Cambridge: Cambridge University Press, 1985.

Scott, Rebecca J., Seymour Drescher, Hebe Maria Mattos, George R. Andrews, and Robert Levine. *The Abolition of Slavery and the Aftermath of Emancipation in Brazil.* Durham, N.C.: Duke University Press, 1988.

Toplin, Robert Brent. *The Abolition of Slavery in Brazil.* New York: Atheneum, 1972.

Index